Trauma Essentials

The Go-To Guide

Trauma Essentials

The Go-To Guide

BABETTE ROTHSCHILD

W.W. NORTON & COMPANY
NEW YORK • LONDON

11|7|11
Lan
$19.95

The author welcomes brief correspondence from readers.
She may be reached at:

Babette Rothschild
PO Box 241778
Los Angeles, CA 90024
Telephone: 310 281 9646
E-mail: babette@trauma.cc, babette@safetraumarecovery.com
Web site: www.trauma.cc, www.safetraumarecovery.com

For information about permission to reproduce selections from this book, write to
Permissions, W. W. Norton & Company, Inc.
500 Fifth Avenue, New York, NY 10110

For information about special discounts for bulk purchases, please contact
W. W. Norton Special Sales at
specialsales@wwnorton.com or 800-233-4830

Manufacturing by RR Donnelley, Bloomsburg
Book design by Gilda Hannah
Production manager: Leeann Graham

Library of Congress Cataloging-in-Publication Data

Rothschild, Babette.
Trauma essentials : the go-to guide / Babette Rothschild.—1st ed.
    p. ; cm.
"A Norton professional book."
Includes bibliographical references and index.
ISBN 978-0-393-70620-8 (pbk.)
1. Post-traumatic stress disorder—Treatment. 2. Traumatic neuroses—
Treatment. I. Title. [DNLM: 1. Stress Disorders, Post-Traumatic. WM 172]
RC552.P67R686 2011
616.85'2106—dc22
                                        2010037265

ISBN: 978-0-393-70620-8 (pbk.)

W. W. Norton & Company, Inc., 500 Fifth Avenue, New York, N.Y. 10110
www.wwnorton.com

W. W. Norton & Company Ltd.,
Castle House, 75/76 Wells Street, London W1T 3QT

1 2 3 4 5 6 7 8 9 0

Contents

Acknowledgments   7

Preface   9

INTRODUCTION
10 Foundations for Safe Trauma Therapy   13

CHAPTER 1
What Is Psychological Trauma?   17

CHAPTER 2
What Is Posttraumatic Stress Disorder?   22

CHAPTER 3
Conditions Associated (or Concurrent) with PTSD   27

CHAPTER 4
How Does Psychological Trauma Affect the Body and Brain?   31

CHAPTER 5
How Is Traumatic Memory Different?   41

CHAPTER 6
Who Does and Does Not Get PTSD?   46

CHAPTER 7
Treating PTSD   56

CHAPTER 8
Current Methods of Trauma Therapy   68

CHAPTER 9
Psychopharmacology for PTSD   84

CHAPTER 10
Mindfulness and Meditation   90

CHAPTER 11
Somatic Treatment Adjuncts   99

CHAPTER 12
How to Tell if a Treatment Works   104

CHAPTER 13
Common Issues Inherent in PTSD   112

CHAPTER 14
What About Prevention?   120

CHAPTER 15
First Aid   126

CHAPTER 16
Vulnerability and Self-Care   132

References   141
Index   147

Acknowledgments

At the top of the list, I want to thank my editor, Deborah Malmud, for asking me to contribute to this series. Per usual, working with her has been fun and enriching. This year marks the 10th that we have been collaborating as editor and author and I hope that we are able to go on as such for another 10 or 20 or 30 to come. Really, Deborah has spoiled me for working with any other editor. From my heart, Deborah, thank you very, very much!

Actually, the whole W. W. Norton family makes the author experience such a pleasure. Thanks also to Libby Burton, Vani Kannan, and Kevin Olsen for your skills and kindness through this project (as well as many others).

I also want to give a special thank you to Trudy Goodman and Christiane Wolf from Insight LA for helping me to better represent mindfulness and meditation in its applications for PTSD. Your feedback was invaluable.

Preface

Since 1980 when posttraumatic stress disorder (PTSD) first appeared as a diagnostic category in the third edition of the Diagnostic and Statistical Manual of Mental Disorders (DSM III) of the American Psychological Association (APA), the number of individuals seeking trauma therapy has grown exponentially. Victims of traumatic events of all types seek treatment for their—often debilitating—symptoms through professional and self-referral. Few practitioners are left wanting for traumatized clients and many specialize in and exclusively treat PTSD. Memberships in the European and International Societies for Traumatic Stress Studies are substantial.

Good psychotherapy, especially trauma therapy, requires a partnership between the therapist and the client. The better informed each is about what they are dealing with and the options for treatment, the greater the chance for a successful outcome. Trauma Essentials is intended as an aid to this therapeutic partnership. Written with both therapist and client in mind, Trauma Essentials presents the most necessary and relevant information in a compact and accessible volume.

Goals of Trauma Treatment

Though this book is filled with theory, options, techniques, and case histories, there is one concept that ought not be lost amid all the words: The first, foremost, and only goal of trauma therapy must always be to improve the quality of life—on a day-to-day basis—of the traumatized individual. It may seem unnecessary to some readers to emphasize this. However, amid the restrictions of managed care, the confusion of the evidence base, and the competition among the drug companies, this basic, essential goal is often overshadowed by other agendas. Therefore, this book, titled and focused on trauma essentials, promotes the quality of life of the trauma survivor as the primary concern and singular aim of any program of trauma recovery. Hopefully that comes across in every chapter. But just in case, it is mentioned again from time to time.

Book Organization

Trauma Essentials: The Go-To Guide is organized into chapters of the most essential trauma topics for both layperson and professional. It is my intention for all readers to be able to easily read through the whole book or refer to individual chapters or sections.

Throughout the book, the cases of Brett and Jeffrey (to be introduced in Chapter 1) will provide a red thread of understanding. Readers will be able to follow even difficult concepts via their increasing familiarity with these two individuals. Additional case material further illustrates ideas and keeps the theory accessible.

Disclaimer

As with all of my books and trainings, I must begin with my disclaimer. That is to say that every model, idea, and notion in this book is theory and speculation. Even though the field of traumatic stress has evolved over the last decades, there are still no hard facts to be found, no truths. I write these words with recognition that even in science and medicine there are few hard facts. Remember, the idea that the earth is round or that it revolves around the sun was controversial at one time; such ideas were even considered heresy. As one of my own physicians told me once, "Today's gospel is tomorrow's heresy, and vice versa."

I feel compelled to begin with this caveat so that you do not take my (or anyone else's) authoritative opinions as completely conclusive. Certainly, just as knowledge in other areas of science and medicine changes and evolves over time, in the area of trauma the same will occur.

Neurologist Antonio Damasio (1994), in his seminal book Descartes' Error, reminds us that in science we have "approximations" that we use until better ones come along. My own way of looking at it is that each of us has only our opinions, along with the experts. It is important not to confuse an opinion with truth. At least in the case of trauma theory no one knows the "truth." So in the following pages I will be sharing with you my own considered opinions as well as the considered opinions of others in the field. I will be taking advantage of the most current and (in my opinion) usable theories and concepts—the best approximations—available to date.

Trauma Essentials

The Go-To Guide

10 Foundations for Safe Trauma Therapy

These 10 foundations for safe trauma therapy were first suggested in The Body Remembers (Rothschild, 2000) and later expanded on in The Body Remembers Casebook (Rothschild, 2003). I include this revised version here, because I believe that these 10 principles are, indeed, essential to any trauma therapy.

1. First and foremost: Establish safety for the client within and outside the therapy.

In Chapter 7, Janet's three-phase approach to trauma therapy is presented. His guiding principle is to prioritize stabilization and safety before working with volatile memories. That wisdom has been a guiding light of common sense for more than 100 years and continues to be. Safe trauma therapy aims to improve a client's quality of life. Stability and ability to function normally in a secure environment are essential to accomplishing all other goals.

2. Develop good contact between therapist and client as a prerequisite to addressing traumatic memories or applying any techniques—even if that takes months or years.

Research continues to demonstrate the importance of the therapeutic relationship (see Chapter 7). This is no different in trauma therapy. In fact, in some cases it will be the most important element. At the very least, a therapeutic alliance is necessary so the client has a secure ally when the going gets tough.

3. Client and therapist must be confident in applying the brakes before they use the accelerator.

"Applying the brakes" has come to be my slogan for working with trauma slowly, with an emphasis on containment. Just like driving a car, safe trauma therapy requires knowing how to stop before speeding ahead. It is unwise to set a volatile process in motion—regardless of the method applied—before clients know how to regulate affect and control flashbacks. They will be safest when they are readily able to calm themselves down even when strongly provoked by their trauma memories (for more on this, see Rothschild, 2000, 2003, 2010a, as well as my "Safe Trauma Recovery" video on Youtube.com).

4. Identify and build on the client's internal and external resources.

When the focus is on trauma, it is easy to forget the accompanying mechanisms that have helped people to survive and carry on, even when they have PTSD. Resources of both the past and present are important allies; they mediate the negative effects of trauma. Resources are partners that make survival and life after trauma possible. Wise therapists will listen as carefully for coping mechanisms as they do for possible trauma. Extracting, developing, and exploiting as many resources as possible will both help clients in their daily lives and make trauma therapy much easier (see Chapter 6).

5. Regard defenses as resources. Never get rid of coping strategies or defenses; instead, create more choices.

By definition, defense mechanisms are coping strategies. They enable us to deal with adversity. They are like old, dependable friends who help us to get through hard times. When they cause us trouble is when they are our only options for dealing with distress. In some cases, the best strategy will actually be to increase a client's defenses, for example, teaching a child how to cope better within his dysfunctional family. At the least, it is a good idea to develop alternative ways to manage so that there is a choice. For instance, many trauma clients complain about dissociation. It can be an inconvenient way to respond to stress, disappearing from thoughts, feelings, or body at (often) inopportune times. However, dissociation can also be a huge help in some situations. How I wish I could dissociate at the dentist in the way that some of my clients are able to do. In no way do I wish to rob them of that important skill. Instead, I want to teach them how to choose whether or not to dissociate at work, with family and friends, and so on (see Chapter 6).

6. View the trauma system as a pressure cooker. Always work to reduce—never to increase—the pressure.

There is a somewhat common misbelief that clients in the freeze state are underaroused; that is, that their nervous systems are working below par. When that is the operating principle, the therapist will work to provoke a frozen client into action. Unfortunately, this can lead to greater dissociation and sometimes panic attacks or worse. Every trauma client, whether frozen, dissociated, or hypervigilant, is suffering with a nervous system that is in overdrive, already provoked to the highest level. Reducing pressure by removing provocation will relieve the nervous system and make mobility, calmness, and clear thinking more possible (see Chapter 4).

7. Adapt the therapy to the client, rather than expecting the client to adapt to the therapy. This requires that the therapist be familiar with several theory and treatment models.

Trauma therapy is really no different than anything else in life in that what appeals and what works will vary from person to person. No one food is palatable (or even nutritious) for all people. No medicine helps everyone. So, of course, there is no method of trauma treatment that will work for every client—or every therapist, for that matter. For that reason, there needs to be options for both professional and consumer. The more methods a therapist has to offer, the more flexibility there will be for the client. Most importantly, if one or more methods fail or are not suitable, the therapist will have others to offer. That will save a lot of difficulty for both therapist and client alike.

8. Have a broad knowledge of theory—both psychology and physiology of trauma and PTSD. This reduces errors and allows the therapist to create techniques tailored to a particular client's needs.

Interventions that a therapist creates for a particular client in a particular moment are the ones that will have the most healing potential. Though learning the protocols of standardized treatment methods can, no doubt, be useful, they are also limiting when only applied as a step-by-step procedure. A good grounding in theory makes not only for a better informed therapist but also a more creative and flexible one. Ideally, every therapy should be tailored to the individual needs of each client. Without understanding theory, this would not be possible.

9. Regard the client's individual differences, and do not judge for noncompliance or for the failure of an intervention. Never expect one intervention to have the same result with two clients.

One of the most disturbing things I hear in trainings and at conferences is therapists blaming their clients for therapeutic failures. Most of the time such accusations are expressed by professionals who expect their clients to fit into narrowly defined treatment parameters. When the client does not fit, they fail. Since no two people are alike, this has never made sense to me. Of course, resistance and other blocks to healing do exist. However, when the therapist is able to work together with the client to tailor a course of therapy, such hindrances minimize. Do not forget, no treatment—of any sort—works for everyone.

10. The therapist must be prepared, at times—or even for a whole course of therapy—to put aside any and all techniques and just talk with the client.

It is so easy to get caught up in our methods and procedures that we sometimes forget the human being that is in the room with us. At times for every client, and all the time for a few clients, it will be the best strategy and the best therapy to be together talking or just sitting quietly.

CHAPTER 1

What is Psychological Trauma?

B elow are introductory sketches of two individuals who developed posttraumatic stress disorder (PTSD) following life-threatening incidents. Throughout the rest of the text, their experiences are used to illustrate various concepts of psychological trauma. The two are revisited often in subsequent chapters and discussed in the context of the ideas being presented. This will provide both therapist and client with a red thread of continuity that will tie the book's theoretical and practical material together.

Two Red-Thread Cases

Brett, a 35-year-old artist, grew up in a loving and supportive home. Her childhood and adolescence were uneventful and she enjoyed her undergraduate college years. However, in her early 20s she experienced an event that would change the felt security and predictability of her life. At 23 she was raped by a criminal psychopath who had escaped from a nearby prison. She eventually sneaked off while he slept, fleeing to the nearest hospital emergency room, which was having a busy night. For undetermined reasons (probably her disheveled and panicked appearance), the hospital staff dismissed her as a psychiatric case. She had to wait more than half an hour before someone listened to her, took her seriously, and called the police and her family. In many ways, those 30 minutes of abandonment in the hospital plagued her more than the actual rape.

Jeffrey was 18 when he enlisted in the U.S. Army, knowing that would mean stretches in both Afghanistan and Iraq. For him it was a good career choice and he wanted to serve his country. He had several friends who had preceded him, all still faring okay. Three weeks into his first tour of duty, the truck he was riding in hit a land mine. He was thrown clear and did not sustain any serious physical injuries. However, three of the other soldiers were not so lucky. Jeffrey ran to their aid but was unable to save them. He and two others watched in horror as their buddies died while waiting for medics to arrive.

Neither Brett nor Jeffrey sustained serious or lasting physical injuries. However, each was profoundly affected and disabled by their experiences, what is known as psychological trauma. How is it that such experiences, despite leaving no visible cuts, bruises, or scars, have an impact that gouges so deeply into the psyche?

The Psychological Impact of Trauma

Psychological trauma is the response of the mind and nervous system to an experience that is so overwhelmingly frightening and life threatening that it cannot come to terms with it. As a result, psychological and psychosomatic symptoms develop at a level that may interfere with normal functioning. Use of the term psychosomatic does not imply that something is being made up or that symptoms are unreal. Instead, it refers to the recognized effect of trauma on the body, via the mind, through the nervous system.

Trauma is generally understood as the response to a traumatic event, an incident that threatens your own life or bodily integrity (both Brett and Jeffrey) or that of another in close proximity or relationship to you (as also with Jeffrey). The discussion of trauma in this book is limited to psychological trauma and therefore, does not include physical trauma (an emergency medical condition), including brain damage (which must be treated neurologically), that may be caused by a traumatic event. Trauma Essentials targets the psychological effects of traumatic events including, but not limited to PTSD.

Stress

Before grasping the concepts of trauma and traumatic stress, it is first necessary to understand what stress itself is. The psychosomatic nature of stress was first identified by Hans Selye (1956, 1984) in his book, The Stress of Life. He defined it simply as the response of any organism to a stressor, a demand. The stressor can actually be either pleasant or unpleasant; it must just be something that requires a degree of effort from the mind (e.g., a school exam) or body (e.g. running a race). A wedding is a common example of a (usually) pleasant event that is often also stressful for the bride and groom. Sexual activity is another example. While sex is usually pleasant for most people, it also exerts demand, and thereby stress, on the body, particularly sexual climax. Additional examples of pleasant stress abound including action and thriller movies, sports, dancing, gardening, mountain climbing, and so on.

Of course, on the other side of the coin is unpleasant stress, the extreme of which would be traumatic stress, stress resulting from a traumatic event. People with PTSD have a chronically high stress level as a result of the disorder. That is why, for a while, those with PTSD may necessarily forego parties, movies, or even sex until their nervous systems become normalized again and they can tolerate more stimulation.

Which Events Are Traumatic?

The first time PTSD appeared as a diagnostic category in DSM-III, the events that could cause it were very narrowly defined. At that time, for an incident to be considered traumatic, it had to be something "that would evoke significant symptoms of distress in almost everyone" (APA, 1980 p.238). By the time the DSM-IV came out in 1994, the definition became much more sensible. The current parameters in the revised DSM-IV-TR (APA, 2000) include incidents that threaten life or physical integrity whether a person experiences something directly, witnesses it happening to another, or hears about it happening to a close friend or relation (e.g., the family and friends of Brett, Jeffrey, and Jeffrey's comrades). According to those criteria, many types and circumstances of incidents could qualify.

There are three main categories of traumatic events: natural events, accidents, and person to person. Examples include:

- Natural events: flood, earthquake, hurricane, tidal wave
- Accidents of all sorts that cause injury: auto, boat, household, falls
- Person to person: assault, rape, torture, physical and sexual abuse, war

This list is not exhaustive, but will give you an idea of what to consider.

Traumatic Stress Versus Other Forms of Stress

I am often asked about other categories of distress, such as emotional abuse. Is this also traumatic stress? While many things can happen to a person that are highly upsetting, to qualify as a traumatic event, the element of threat or harm to life or body must be present. This distinction is central to the DSM criteria, and it also makes sense. Traumatic stress, the reaction to a life-threatening event, pushes arousal in the nervous system to the extreme responses of flight, fight, and freeze. While other types of stressors can be very, very upsetting, it is the release of these survival responses that distinguishes trauma from other forms of stress.

Of course, an individual's perception of the threat level of an event would be a pertinent factor in making this distinction. Say five people are riding in the same car when it swerves and crashes into a tree, with everyone surviving. One or more of the passengers may have feared for their lives while others never worried they would be seriously hurt or killed. In that case, the nervous systems of those who did perceive their lives to be in danger would activate traumatic stress while the others would have lower levels of stress.

So while an incident or issue may be pressing or disconcerting, it may not be trauma. Of course, such encounters need consideration and attention nonetheless. Just because something does not qualify as trauma does not in any way imply that it is not important. Sometimes when the focus is on trauma it can seem that other things are not worthy of attention. It is relevant for anyone dealing with trauma to keep in mind that nontraumatic distress still warrants notice.

What Is Normal in Response to Trauma?

When confronted with a threat to life or limb, there are limited choices for response. The same options exist throughout the animal kingdom, including primates and humans. You have probably heard of the three survival reflexes: flight, fight, and freeze. All three are normal. All three are determined (usually) via the limbic system, the survival center of the brain.

Flight involves running away or escaping via another means. The function of this response is to remove the individual from the threat. Flight is usually the first line of defense. Fight is an attempt to fend off a perpetrator or attacker. The last resort is the freeze response. The limbic system will direct the body to freeze when flight or fight are not possible or the body is not capable.

So, for example, if you notice someone threatening following too closely, speeding up, breaking into a run, or ducking into a shop could be a defensive response. Likewise, for someone who is strong enough, fending off an attack by human or animal can be the best strategy. When neither of those is possible, the freeze response (which can look like playing dead) could save a life. Chapter 4 expands on these concepts in the context of neurobiology.

Conclusion

Psychological trauma is just that, psychological. Though sometimes a traumatized individual also has physical trauma (that is, injuries), it may be the psychological consequences of trauma that have the deepest and most enduring consequences. In the next chapter, the most extreme psychological consequence of trauma, PTSD, is defined and discussed in detail.

CHAPTER 2

What is Posttraumatic Stress Disorder?

Normally, we know that memories recall our past. When we reflect on a birthday party, learning to drive, or college graduation, we are clear that we are, indeed, remembering something that happened some expanse of time ago. Such recollections do not cause us to fully feel as though we are 6, 16, or 22 again though we might have flashes of such. In addition, most of that kind of remembering is done voluntarily, for example, when talking to someone or looking at photos. It is rare for normal memories to suddenly invade and preoccupy our minds and bodies uninvited.

However, something quite different happens with PTSD: The memory of a traumatic event does not rest easily in the past. The trauma survivor feels as though the incident recurs or continues on and on. Moreover, it can intrude into consciousness, unbidden, often disrupting the usual flow of daily life. Here are a few examples:

- The war veteran dives for cover when hearing a car backfire or a jet take off from a nearby airport. For several minutes he is panicked, convinced he is back in the trenches dodging enemy fire.
- The assault victim walks nervously through every neighbor-

hood—no matter how safe—with heart beating just as fast as it did on the day she was attacked.
- The tsunami survivor wakes screaming from recurrent nightmares, overwhelmed by reexperiencing the perception of being pulled under and suffocated in the water.

To correct this memory distortion, the bottom line for PTSD therapy (see Chapter 7) is to help traumatized clients to realize—in their entire being, mind and body—their trauma is over. They survived. What has been plaguing them since that time is a memory of the past.

Terminology Basics

Several diagnoses are actually relevant for understanding trauma. The next chapter concentrates on associated conditions that can be confused with or appear concurrent with problems related to trauma. However, the two that are the most trauma-specific are addressed in this chapter:

- Posttraumatic stress disorder (PTSD)
- Acute stress disorder (ASD)

Both of these diagnoses are (and always have been) categorized under anxiety disorders in the Diagnostic and Statistical Manual of Mental Disorders of the American Psychiatric Association (APA). At this writing, the current volume of this important reference is the fourth edition "Text Revision" (DSM-IV-TR) (APA, 2000). The latest prediction of the due date for DSM-V is 2013, according to http://www.dsm5.org.

There is a second reference for psychological diagnosis, the fifth chapter of the 10th edition of the World Health Organization's (2007) International Classification of Diseases, Classification of Mental and Behavioural Disorders. However, since the DSM appears to be the most widely used in English-speaking countries (Andrews, Slade, and Peters, 1999) all definitions and criteria in this book are drawn from the DSM-IV-TR unless otherwise indicated. For anyone interested in closely comparing the two references, see Cross-walks ICD-10/DSM-IV-TR: A Synopsis of Classifications of Mental Disorders (Schulte-Markwort, Marutt, and Riedesser, 2003).

You will find the term posttraumatic spelled with and without a hyphen between the two ts. If you are searching for information or locating books on the Internet, in a bookstore, or at your library, you would do best to search both spellings. However, usage in this volume adheres to the spelling in the DSM-IV-TR as well as the Web-site for the National Center for PTSD (http://www.ncptsd.va.gov), neither of which use the hyphen.

Definition

According to the DSM-IV-TR, to qualify for a diagnosis of PTSD a person must have "experienced, witnessed, or been confronted with an event or events that involve actual or threatened death or serious injury, or a threat to the physical integrity of oneself or others." In adults, the person's response must have "involved intense fear, helplessness, or horror" and in children may include "disorganized or agitated behavior" (APA, 2000 p.467). In other words, an individual does not have to be the direct victim of a traumatic event for it to have lasting psychological impact. Watching or hearing about the death or serious injury of someone else carries the same risk.

Merely the experience or initial reaction to a traumatic event does not determine PTSD. What sets it apart from normal responses to trauma is the cluster of symptoms that persist long after the event has ceased and the typically associated reactions should have disappeared, including the following:

- Involuntarily recalling the incident through intrusive images, thoughts, dreams, hallucinations, flashbacks, and triggers
- Avoidance of reminders of the traumatic event that may restrict thought processes, emotional expression, relationships, and activities or even block some or all of the memory of the event
- Persistent hyperarousal that may include an exaggerated startle reflex, trouble concentrating, and sleep disturbances
- Compromise of daily life quality including disruption of contact with friends or family, or ability to function normally in responsible roles (work, child care, school, etc.)

Symptoms must be present for at least 1 month to qualify as PTSD. When they continue for up to 3 months, the PTSD is considered acute. The condition is regarded as chronic if the symptoms persist longer than 3 months. There is also the possibility of delayed-onset PTSD when symptoms emerge at least 6 months following an event (APA, 2000). Delayed-onset PTSD may also include disturbances first arising in adulthood that have roots in childhood trauma.

Incidence

Contrary to what you might think from the amount of coverage on television news, talk shows, and books, PTSD is not a necessary, or even usual, result of traumatic events. In fact, only about 20–25% of people who experience such incidents actually develop PTSD. That means that 75–80% do not (Breslau, Davis, Andreski, & Peterson, 1991; Elliott, 1997; Kulka et al., 1990). So just because someone has been involved in a traumatic incident does not at all mean that he will develop PTSD.

Acute Stress Disorder

A second diagnostic category is sometimes applied in the immediate aftermath of traumatic events. ASD looks pretty much the same as PTSD; it has basically the same origins and symptoms. However, there is this important difference: ASD is short lived. That is, the symptoms resolve within a month or so. If symptoms persist beyond that first month, then the diagnosis changes to PTSD.

Distinguishing PTSD and ASD From Other Diagnoses

One of the main features that distinguishes both PTSD and ASD from other diagnoses in the DSM is that they are 100% event dependent. Without an identifiable event, neither of those diagnoses applies. This means that no matter how many of the symptoms of PTSD or ASD a particular person exhibits, if no precipitating traumatizing event can be identified, then the diagnosis must be something else with similar symptoms (see chapter 3 for possibilities).

Sometimes both therapists and clients find this constraint to be limiting and frustrating. However, it is actually very protective of the client. In general, rigorous diagnosis should help to guide responsible treatment. When no event can be found to account for symptoms, then the symptoms must be treated for their own sake rather than trying to uncover memories in the hopes of locating an event that may or may not exist. Restricting the diagnosis of PTSD and ASD to clients who have experienced recognizable causal events helps to safeguard them from the risk of creating false memories to account for symptoms, something that is very dangerous to anyone's mental health. See Chapter 13 for a more in-depth discussion of this common risk factor.

As ASD and PTSD are basically the same disorder in different phases of its course, when referring to PTSD through the rest of this book, the reader may assume that the discussion includes ASD.

Diagnosing Brett and Jeffrey

In the immediate aftermath of the rape, it appeared that Brett only suffered ASD. The nervousness and crying spells that followed that ordeal abated after about 3.5 weeks. She returned to her graduate studies and no longer talked about her experience. She seemed okay. However, 12 years later, while making love with her new fiancé, she had a flashback of the rape and became inconsolable. She was unable to go to work for the next week or to let her fiancé touch her in any amorous way. At the end of that week she sought the help of a psychotherapist who gave her the diagnosis of delayed-onset PTSD.

Jeffrey's situation was different. His immediate symptoms of hypervigilance, recurring cold sweats, sleep disturbance, and weight loss, coupled with continuing visions of his buddies dying, persisted long after the first month. Over the next few years he was in and out of the Veterans Administrtion psychiatric hospitals, bearing an obvious diagnosis of PTSD.

CHAPTER 3

Conditions Associated (or Concurrent) with PTSD

There are many psychological difficulties that are routinely mistaken for, associated with, or present concurrently with PTSD. The main ones include the following:

- Other anxiety disorders
- Dissociative disorders
- Borderline personality disorder (BPD)
- Attachment disorder
- Substance abuse
- Traumatic brain injury (TBI)

Other Anxiety Disorders

PTSD has always been categorized with the anxiety disorders in the DSM. Additional diagnoses relevant to PTSD in this category include panic attack, panic disorder, agoraphobia, phobias, obsessive-compulsive disorder, and generalized anxiety disorder. Major physiological symptoms of PTSD include elevated heart and respiration rates. This is due to a persistent stress response in the autonomic nervous system. Anxiety and panic attacks in particular also exhibit similar elevations. So it might sometimes be difficult to determine if a panic attack is due to trauma or another type of stressor unless the precise trigger can be identified. That said, there is also relevant speculation as to whether any or all of these conditions have traumatic roots. Perhaps one day there will be a category of traumatic stress disorders with the conditions above (and maybe below also) included under that umbrella category.

Dissociative Disorder

The concept of dissociation refers to a splitting or disconnection between elements of the self or psyche. There is an ongoing debate among professionals who specialize in trauma research and treatment as to whether PTSD is, as mentioned above, an anxiety disorder or if it is more likely to be a dissociative disorder. Dissociation is a common feature of PTSD and is at the root of many of its symptoms, including flashbacks (intense memories that feel as if one is reliving the experience). Moreover, there is speculation that dissociation during or following a trauma may predict the development of PTSD (Bremner et al., 1992; Briere, Scott, & Weathers, 2005; Classen, Koopman, & Spiegel, 1993). Actually, it is probably most likely that PTSD comprises strong elements from both anxiety and dissociative disorders. I have often speculated that in the future there could be a shift in the understanding of these disorders resulting in anxiety disorders, dissociative disorders, and other conditions falling under the major category of PTSD.

The dissociative disorders seen most commonly with PTSD are dissociative amnesia (psychological disconnection from some or all memories), dissociative identity disorder (more commonly known as multiple personality disorder), and depersonalization (psychological disconnection from feeling one's body).

Borderline Personality Disorder

BPD is characterized by a long history of unstable relationships and labile (volatile or quickly changing) emotions. There is a reasonably sound body of literature suggesting that BPD has significant roots in trauma, particularly physical or sexual abuse in early childhood (APA, 2000; Herman & van der Kolk, 1987; Gunderson & Sabo, 1993; among others). Many people with BPD suffer symptoms concurrent with PTSD, particularly flashbacks. Most professionals I have come in contact with assume that a client with BPD also has a trauma history involving some kind of intrusion or boundary violation, whether or not reported or remembered.

Attachment Disorder

Attachment theory is probably the fastest-growing area of study in the psychotherapy branch of psychology. The foundational premise asserts the importance of the primary infant-caregiver relationship. When that goes well, individuals develop resilience that assists them in adjusting to and coping with the stresses of life, including traumatic stress. When that primary relationship does not go well, an individual can be more vulnerable to psychological disturbances from all types of stress, particularly traumatic stress. Really, the psychological and psychotherapy community have always known this. However, we now have hard neuropsychological data from attachment studies that confirm it. Commonly, in those people whose trauma began very early in life, and particularly when trauma was perpetrated by a primary caregiver, attachment disorder is a likely consequence concurrent with PTSD.

Substance Abuse

Dual diagnosis is the common term applied to substance abusers (drug addicts and others) who have additional psychological problems, often PTSD. It can be a vicious circle for these individuals: the fright, horror, and shame associated with trauma drive them to substance abuse. In turn, addiction makes healing from trauma much, much more difficult.

Traumatic Brain Injury

TBI involves purely physical damage as the result of a severe blow or other insult to the head, wounding not just the cranial bones but also the brain inside. TBI can result from either accident or violence and can be life threatening or even fatal. Still, many individuals survive TBI with greater and lesser degrees of physical and emotional handicap associated with their injuries. TBI is often categorized with PTSD, often being paired as conference or training themes, particularly with regard to returning combat veterans. This can be a bit confusing as the symptom profiles and treatment options are somewhat different for each, particularly because resulting changes in the brain may render traditional PTSD methods, intended for treatment of the psychological symptoms, weakened or useless. Of course there may be overlaps as TBI can be emotionally distressing for both the victim and the family. In addition, depending on the location and severity of the damage, TBI may also interfere with emotional regulation itself. In general, the treatment for the psychological consequences of TBI requires additional interventions that are beyond the scope of this book on the essentials of psychological trauma. I mention TBI here only to make this clarification. Dealing with TBI is an important topic worthy of separate in-depth attention.

Additional Diagnosis for Jeffrey

Though Brett's diagnosis was purely PTSD, Jeffrey qualified for one of the concurrent conditions described above. As is typical with many traumatized war veterans, for a time Jeffrey sought refuge in narcotics and alcohol. Technically, then, he qualifies for dual diagnosis: PTSD and substance abuse. Though eventually he ceased the use of these substances during his course of trauma treatment, he continued to qualify for the dual diagnosis because of his continued involvement with Alcoholics Anonymous and Narcotics Anonymous.

CHAPTER 4

How Does Psychological Trauma Affect the Body and Brain?

As with many who suffer from trauma, the somatic disturbances were among the most disconcerting symptoms for both Brett and Jeffrey. Brett suffered sleep disturbances, tachycardia (rapid heartbeat), dysregulated appetite (times of over- and undereating), and periods of vertigo. She also had intense visual and sensory flashbacks, particularly if her fiancé unexpectedly touched her in the dark. Generally, except for the appetite irregularities, her symptoms flared primarily at night. During the day Brett functioned relatively normally. She held a responsible job and was able to manage household chores including shopping, cooking, and cleaning.

Jeffrey, on the other hand, had more pervasive symptoms, affecting him throughout the course of a normal day: concentration difficulties, sweats, nervousness, and so on. However, the symptom Jeffrey found the most difficult to deal with was his intense feelings of guilt. He had lived when his buddies had not and his survivor guilt was extremely difficult to bear.

Why is it that so many years after the original events, Brett and Jeffrey both continued suffering to such a great degree? How is it that their bodies and minds perpetuated the experience of trauma, diminishing the quality of their lives and compromising their relationships? The discussion in this chapter provides some understanding.

Stress: The Core of Posttraumatic Stress Disorder

Since the beginning of trauma studies in the latter part of the 20th century, it has been recognized that trauma, traumatic stress, acute stress disorder and PTSD all have a significant effect on the body as well as on the brain. It is no accident that the central word of the diagnostic term PTSD is stress, a recognized psychobiological condition first described by Hans Selye in the 1950s:

> For scientific purposes, stress is defined as the nonspecific response of the body to any demand [stressor]. It was first recognized by evidence of adrenal stimulation, shrinkage of lymphatic organs, gastrointestinal ulcers, and loss of body weight with characteristic alterations in the chemical composition of the body." (1956–1984, p.74)

Stress initiates activation in the nervous system to enable the body to meet whatever demand is encountered. Though generally regarded as a response to a negative experience, it is important to remember that stress can also result from positive experiences such as marriage, job change, moving, gardening, exercise, sexual activity, and so on.

That the mind and body could experience stress from activities that one would normally consider fun, pleasant, or exciting can be very helpful for the traumatized individual to understand. Everyone has their own personal threshold for how much stress can be managed at any one time. When the personal stress level exceeds that threshold, problems occur. Difficulties can range from simple anxiety on the lower end to complete collapse or decompensation on the most debilitating end. People with normally balanced nervous systems (that is, not disrupted by PTSD) manage the fluctuations of stress levels during the day and throughout their lives. Stress goes up, stress goes down. However, persons with PTSD have decreased capacity for this easy (and usually unconscious) modulation. Such individuals live with a baseline level of stress that is far greater than that of the nontraumatized person. The latter may have periods of no stress at all, with a baseline at zero. However, for the individual with trauma, the base stress level is already quite high. For that reason, many trauma survivors are not able to tolerate increasing their level of stress, no matter how fun or pleasurable an activity might be. Often they can no longer enjoy some of the activities that they used to, such as exciting movies, parties, or a jog in the park. This can be very discouraging and difficult to accept.

It may help to understand that, basically, stress is just stress. The traumatized nervous system and the mind do not seem able to distinguish pleasant from unpleasant stress when the base level has reached a particular intensity. So once-desirable pastimes become undesirable, at least for a while. Those individuals who understand that their chronically elevated stress level cannot tolerate being pushed higher often are better able to ride out the healing process. As their traumatic stress resolves, normal activities will again feel normal. This morsel of psychoeducation can give trauma survivors confidence that, eventually, they will be able to get back to enjoying pleasantly stressful pursuits again as they heal from their trauma.

Metered doses of theory, per the above example, can be helpful to many who are suffering the effects of trauma. Below are additional portions of theory that can be useful to therapist and client alike. Grasping how trauma works on and with the nervous system will aid the helping professional to facilitate the patient's healing.

The Brain

It would take many volumes to thoroughly discuss the brain in total. In this book I will stick to an overview discussion of the parts of the brain that are most relevant to the essential understanding of trauma: the cortex (the thinking center of the brain) and the limbic system (the emotional and survival center of the brain).

The Cortex

Among other functions, the cortex is the site of conscious thought and awareness. Maintaining attention to our external environment (what we see, hear, smell, etc.) as well as our internal environment (thoughts, body sensations, and emotions) requires activity in the cortex. Thinking, including the recall of facts, description of procedures, recognition of time, understanding, and so on, also take place in the cortex. Though it varies from individual to individual, low levels of increased stress with the accompanying increase in adrenaline levels will actually improve awareness, clear thinking, and memory.* That is why

---

* Adrenaline and noradrenaline are the familiar names for the hormones epinephrine and norepinephrine. In the United States, the latter terms are more usual in scientific texts. However, in Europe and elsewhere, it is the more familiar usage that predominates. Because this book is written for both therapists and clients, and will be read on both sides of the Atlantic Ocean, adrenaline and noradrenaline are used throughout.

coffee is such a popular beverage at work and among university students: a jolt of caffeine makes our memory, observations, and thinking processes sharper. However, past a certain (individually determined) level, increased adrenaline will degrade, that is, have the opposite effect on, those same processes. A most recognizable example is seen on television quiz programs. More often than not, contestants eliminated by a wrong answer will assert that when watching the program at home, they never missed an answer. Why then were they stumped when on TV? Most likely, their stress levels rose beyond the helpful low-adrenaline kick and succumbed to overload that dampened their ability to access information that was easily available under calmer circumstances. The same thing can happen with trauma. Though many survivors report a sharpening of perception and thought, those with PTSD usually have a different experience. In such cases, their brains became overloaded with adrenaline and they were no longer able to think clearly as they ran, fought, or—most likely—froze in response to the traumatic threat. Understanding the interaction of the cortex with the limbic system during low and high stress will help to make this loss of cortex ability clearer.

The Limbic System

Located in the middle part of the brain between the brain stem and cortex, the limbic system is responsible for our survival. It protects us from danger in major part by recognizing and utilizing sensory information and then setting in motion the protective responses of flight, fight, and freeze. The limbic system assesses the states of both internal and external environments via sensory input and transfers the data to other brain structures. The amygdala is the limbic structure that assigns the sensory information an emotional interpretation and instructs the body in how to respond accordingly. For instance, while waiting at the train station for your friend to arrive, you might already be smiling as your amygdala identifies her familiar posture and gait from a distance. In nervous system time, your smiling response appears long before you have consciously recognized her face as she approaches. On the other end of the spectrum, it is also the amygdala that evaluates sensory information (what is seen, heard, smelled, etc.) as comprising danger. In such an instance it will raise an alarm and instruct the body to respond quite differently, to run away or dive for cover (flight), fend off (fight), or go numb or faint (freeze).

Another structure in the limbic system, the hippocampus, is very important for managing, remembering, and recovering from trauma. Among other things, it is the hippocampus that registers and then informs the cortex about the time context of an event. It marks the memory of each event with a beginning, middle, and end. For example, remember a simple episode from yesterday: a meal, a phone call, taking a shower, whatever. As you bring to mind the details, notice whether you recall how the incident began, what happened during it, and then the end of it.

As I am writing this page right now, I am remembering teaching my elderly neighbor how to use his new cellular telephone—the first one he had ever owned. It started with my knocking on his front door. He welcomed me in. Then, we went through the various steps of using the phone. I programmed some speed dial numbers for him and he wrote down how to find them. Then after about an hour, we were finished. He said, "Thanks!" I said, "You're welcome. Just don't forget to turn it on!" He let me out the door.

My memory of the details in sequence are due to the hippocampus doing its job. It will usually do that for any event, recording and then telling the cortex when it started, how long it proceeded, and that it finished.

Take special note of that last step of hippocampal sequencing, recording that an event has ended. With regard to remembering trauma, this is vitally important. In fact, typically PTSD is the result of a hippocampus that was not able to mark the end of the trauma. It was never able to tell the cortex that the trauma ended. Such a failure of the hippocampus is really the crux of PTSD, perhaps even the major cause. When the hippocampus is able to recognize and tell the cortex that a traumatic event has concluded, the cortex can then instruct the amygdala that the trauma is over. Once informed, the amygdala can then halt its alarm response, telling the body there is no further need for hypervigilance or flight, fight, or freeze. That is what happens when a trauma is resolved—whether at the time or in the near or distant future. The hippocampus recognizes the end of it and informs the cortex, which in turn alerts the amygdala to stop all the defensive action. In fact, it is this feature of hippocampal function that makes trauma recovery possible. Without it, the amygdala will go on responding as if the trauma continues again and again and again, which is exactly what is happening when the system fails and PTSD develops. In that case, the hippocampus fails to mark the end of the event, it is not able to inform the cortex, and the amygdala's alarm persists.

While the amygdala is immune to the rise in stress hormones that accompanies traumatic stress, the hippocampus is not so lucky. It is very vulnerable to high levels of stress hormones and will stop working correctly when adrenaline and other hormones reach a high level. Stress arousal needs to be lowered before the hippocampus will have a chance to function properly again.

The Twins of Information Processing

Joseph LeDoux (1996) distinguished two pathways for the processing of sensory information. Both are very speedy in real time. Nonetheless, in the context of nervous system time, one is very fast and the other is rather slow. The first, the quick route, is via the amygdala and bypasses the cortex altogether. The amygdala takes in sensory information from both internal and external environments (see the next section) and tells the body what to do, how to respond. For example, hearing the voice of a loved one on the phone may cause you to sigh deeply before you've even realized who it is and said hello. The amygdala hears the voice, recognizes it as familiar, and associates it with pleasant experience. It does the same with noxious sensory information as well. For example, the smell of smoke may have your heart accelerating long before you have discovered the source. The amygdala registers the smell of smoke, associates it with potential danger, and then prepares the body for defensive action by raising the heart rate. In this quick route of information processing, these reactions are set in motion instantly, long before the possibility for any cortical involvement.

The second, slower route utilizes the hippocampus to send information to the frontal cortex where it can be evaluated with conscious thought. In the two examples in the previous paragraph, this is how it would work. Hearing the voice of the loved one, the hippocampus sends information to the prefrontal cortex that makes possible the identification of who the person is, when you last heard from or saw that person, and any other vital information. On the other hand, when smelling smoke, the hippocampus would relay that information to the cortex where action could be set in motion to discover the source of the smoke or to determine that there is no danger either because the smoke has ceased or because the source was benign.

Survival in life, particularly when dealing with trauma, requires that both of these systems be working properly. However, the high levels of stress hormones, primarily adrenaline, associated with PTSD tend to disable the hippocampus along the slower processing route. When arousal goes up past a certain threshold, the hippocampus stops functioning. When that happens during a traumatic incident, the time sequencing will not be accurately recorded, if it is recorded at all. That means that memory of the event will be devoid of structure: no beginning, no middle, and—critically—no end. In such an instance, the amygdala continues to call an alarm as if the trauma is continuing on and on or again and again. The cortex never received the message that it was over, so it cannot tell the amygdala to calm down. The result is that the person with PTSD is plagued by the persistent reactions of the amygdala to the past danger.

There are some who believe that this hippocampal failure is pathological, a sign of something wrong. However, shutting down the hippocampus is actually part of the survival response. When one's life is in danger, it may be critical to be able to react without thinking. That's the amygdala's job. If the hippocampus remains active at such a threatening time, it could hamper the autopilot and speed necessary for survival. So the amygdala raises the level of stress hormones and the hippocampus goes off-line, so to speak. Still, the shutdown is supposed to be temporary and problems arise when it persists. The hippocampus is meant to come fully back online once the trauma is past, informing the cortex that it is all over. When that doesn't happen, PTSD results.

Trauma recovery involves, in part, turning the hippocampus and the slower information processing route on once again. Once that is accomplished, the cortex, with the aid of the hippocampus, will be able to recognize that the trauma is no longer occurring and in turn will tell the amygdala to halt its constant alarm. A successful outcome will usually see the physical symptoms that have been caused by the amygdala's constant alarm (e.g., palpitations, concentration difficulties, nervousness) subside.

Central Nervous System

The central nervous system is the control center for all body and mind systems. The term is used interchangeably to refer to both the body's entire nervous system and also to the central part of the nervous system, the brain and spinal cord. The nerves that emanate from the spinal cord are divided into two major classifications, those that direct the motor nervous system and the ones connected to the sensory nervous system.

Sensory Nervous System

The motor nervous system (see the next section) usually gets the most attention in books and training on trauma and PTSD, particularly the autonomic nervous system. However, the sensory nervous system holds many keys for understanding how the limbic system, particularly the amygdala, responds to trauma. As well, working directly with the sensory nervous system can help many trauma survivors to get their footing firmly back into the safety of the here and now.

There are two categories of sensory nerves: exteroceptive and interoceptive. The exteroceptors are nerves of the five senses: sight, hearing, taste, touch, and smell. These are the senses that gather information from the environment external to our bodies. The other category, the interoceptors, get input from our internal environment: balance, internal sensations, and the ability to locate all parts of our body without looking (proprioception).

Paying attention to the sensory nervous system can be extremely important when endeavoring to resolve trauma. It is the information from the senses that the amygdala uses to determine whether an environment is safe or dangerous and how to respond (smile, run, and so on).

A common habit of those who suffer from PTSD, as well as panic and anxiety disorders, is their tendency to place a disproportionate amount of emphasis on their interoceptive sensations. This is understandable from the standpoint that all of those conditions bear with them highly uncomfortable physical sensations (e.g., rapid heart rate, dizziness). However, problems arise when the individual uses those discomforting internal sensations to judge the safety or danger of the external environment. In these instances, individuals forget to use their exteroceptors, their senses of sight, hearing, smell, and so on, to actually evaluate a current situation. They may be so overwhelmed by heart palpitations, for example, that they assume what is going on is dangerous without actually knowing if that is the case. This can develop into a kind of trap, survivors assuming that this or that situation is dangerous because of what they are feeling on the inside. It is a deceptive process. In reality, one is safest when able to use exteroceptors to evaluate a situation or environment, but for some trauma survivors, this is a difficult concept to grasp and a challenging process to teach. The way out of this dilemma is to develop a dual awareness (Rothschild, 2000) that will make possible paying attention to both internal and external senses simultaneously.

Motor Nervous System
All muscles are part of the motor nervous system. There are two divi-

sions, the somatic and the autonomic. Muscles of the somatic nervous system are the skeletal muscles, each of which reaches across a joint. Movement is made possible through the contraction and relaxation of the muscles that move the bones on either side of the joint either nearer to or more distant from each other. For example, to chew a piece of gum, the jaw muscles must alternate contraction and relaxation. This makes movement possible between the upper and lower jawbones by in turn bringing them closer together and then farther apart again. Any muscle that facilitates an action (walking, writing) or prevents an action (holds back an impulse) is part of the somatic nervous system.

The autonomic nervous system comprises the viscera and visceral muscles, such as the heart, lungs, and intestines. While most action in the somatic nervous system can be conscious or voluntary, the autonomic nervous system functions automatically. In fact, it is sometimes called the automatic nervous system as most of the time it is functioning outside of our awareness.

Both the autonomic and somatic nervous systems are involved in response to trauma. When confronted with a threat, the amygdala will direct the autonomic nervous system to arouse the body to defensive action. It does this through the hormones of adrenaline and noradrenaline, which increase heart rate and respiration to send lots of oxygen to the muscles (somatic nervous system). This makes possible either strong and quick movement for flight or fight, or paralysis of the muscles (either stiff or slack) for the protective freeze response.

When not in a state of stress, the amygdala will direct the autonomic nervous system to wind down body responses, slowing heart and breath and directing blood flow to the viscera to aid digestion and elimination. In that state, muscles are more relaxed (as opposed to slack) and rest and restoration are possible.

The Role of Cortisol

In the past few years, the role of cortisol in response to and recovery from trauma has become confused. Because it is part of the entire scenario of response to trauma, indeed a stress hormone, cortisol has become erroneously regarded by many as something that increases stress. This is actually not the case and a simple surveying of cortisol research, particularly that by Rachel Yehuda and colleagues (1990, 1995), who first discovered the role of cortisol in trauma, clarifies the matter. With regard to the trauma response, cortisol is a vital friend. The discussion of the amygdala and hippocampus focused on what happens to lay the groundwork for the development of PTSD. The picture is quite different in the scenario that leads in the other direction, to resolution.

When a traumatic situation has ended and the individual has survived through flight or fight, the amygdala directs the adrenal glands to release cortisol to dampen the trauma response. Cortisol halts the arousal and helps the autonomic nervous system to swing from a state of stress to a state of calm. In fact, one of the difficulties for people with PTSD is that their cortisol levels are lower than usual. Cortisol has not been able to do its job for them. In years past, attempts were made to inject those with PTSD with cortisol in the hope that it would be able to do the same after the fact. However, none of these studies showed much promise for a delayed introduction of cortisol.

For those interested in the role of cortisol in other conditions, look particularly to studies on depression. It appears that those suffering from depression typically have raised levels of cortisol. If diagnosis is in doubt, simply assessing cortisol levels will point to an individual's greater tendency toward depression or PTSD (Yehuda et al., 1996).

CHAPTER 5

How Is Traumatic Memory Different?

The primary hallmark of PTSD is the distortion of memory that accompanies it. Sometimes a traumatic event is completely forgotten. Often the incident is remembered, though incompletely or in fragments. However, one characteristic of memory in someone with PTSD particularly distinguishes the disorder. What keeps traumatized people suffering is the phenomenon that their minds and bodies have not been able to put the events they endured into the past. For them, there is no conclusion to the incident—it feels as though it either goes on and on or that it repeats unendingly. The evidence for such an impression is readily observed and felt in the continuing hyperarousal of the trauma survivor's nervous system that sets in motion the flashbacks and other symptoms of the disorder. As a result, a survivor's amygdalae continue to react as if the traumatic threat persists, provoking the autonomic nervous system again to the state of flight, fight, or freeze—whichever was activated at the original time of the trauma. An overview of how normal memory works will help in understanding what goes awry in trauma memory.

Normal Memory

Knowledge of the workings of the brain and memory greatly accelerated in the later part of the 20th century and into the 21st. It is only a few decades since the discovery that revolutionized the way memory was understood. It is now believed that memory processes are organized into two main systems, the implicit and the explicit. Each matures at its own rate, has its own processes, and works together with diverse areas of the brain.

Implicit

The implicit memory system is nonverbal, automatic, and mostly un-conscious. Sometimes it is called procedural memory. It is this type of recall that is activated when we hop on a bicycle and ride it without thinking about what we are doing. As a matter of fact, in writing this book I am dependent on implicit memory. It makes it possible for my fingers to quickly hit the correct letters on my computer keyboard. Without implicit memory, each paragraph would take a very long time to hammer out as I hunted for one letter at a time. All I have to do is think of a word and (usually) my fingers automatically hit the correct keys. The implicit system makes a direct link between my brain and fingers; once I have learned where the keys are, I don't forget.

Thus, the implicit memory system is very efficient. Once a procedure is learned, it becomes automatic and you rarely have to think much about it again. This automatic feature functions the same for distress-ing procedures as well as pleasant, convenient, and time-saving ones. For example, if you learned when you were growing up to withdraw for protection anytime there was conflict, your implicit memory sys-tem may cause you to withdraw, even sometimes unconsciously or in-appropriately, as this will tend to be your automatic response. See the section on traumatic memory, below, for discussion of implicit trauma reactions.

Implicit memory appears to be available at least from birth, possi-bly earlier. It is dependent on the amygdala's role of information gath-ering through the senses, particularly the interoceptors, though the exteroceptive senses can play a role. Emotions (and the sensations that comprise them) are part of this system, as is any kind of conditioning (per the withdrawal example, above).

My good friend and colleague Michael Gavin (whom I have men-tioned in several previous books) recently told me a stunning example of implicit memory recall that he experienced:

Some years ago I was on my way to a business meeting in a part of London I had not visited since I lived there in my later teens. Looking around for the meeting place, I became aware quite suddenly of an intense and puzzling set of feelings and sensations: my heart was beating fast and I felt flushed and tingling. I was aware of excitement, anxiety, and anticipation that was at once pleasant and uneasy. It was bewildering. I felt somehow possessed. Still scanning the street scene, I noticed with a shock of recognition the frontage of a restaurant (amazingly) unchanged in 40 years. It was the restaurant to which, aged 18, I took the girl I was then in love with to dinner. My first love, my first time taking a girl to dinner. As I made the connection, I also began to make sense of the mixture of emotions—eager anticipation, fear of embarrassment, elation and anxiety, desire and diffidence—that were coursing through me once again. I was glad that I was able to take the time to spot the trigger for the experience, which I certainly had not consciously recognized the first time I looked around. Otherwise the impact of 18-year-old emotions on my nearly 60-year-old system would have left me thinking I was a bit crazy. As it was, I was able to enjoy the experience, with just a tinge of wistfulness about all the years that had passed since.

Such is the power of the implicit memory system. It records body sensations and emotions and feeds them back to us when triggered. Often we can identify the source and there is not much disruption. The smell of a familiar food, the sight of a loved one, hearing an old song, and so on. But when the provoked sensations are unpleasant or even frightening, identifying the trigger may or may not be easily accomplished. See Traumatic Memory, below.

Explicit

The explicit memory system becomes available later than the implicit. It is usually not completely functioning until a child reaches her third year. Development of the explicit memory system accompanies the maturation of both the hippocampus (in the limbic system) and spoken language. Sometimes the term episodic is substituted for explicit as one of the explicit system's main functions is to construct narratives of events. That is, "This happened first, then that happened, and the culmination was," and so on. The explicit system is also at work when your recall involves words: a song, a recipe, a list of instructions, steps to accomplish a task, description of an event, recitation of facts, and so on.

Central to explicit memory is the functioning of both the hippocampus and the cortex. The hippocampus, in large part, transmits features of time (when) and space (where) to the cortex. It also plays a role in transmitting other details or facts that are relevant. The discussion in the previous chapter highlighted the importance of the hippocampus in remembering the sequence of an event, the start, middle, and end. This is how the events of our lives get laid down in a timeline. For example, you have explicit memories that you went to high school before you bought your first house. You know that is the correct sequence because of the proper function of the hippocampus within the explicit system.

Traumatic Memory
The stress hormones released during a traumatic incident may greatly affect just how you remember that event. During a traumatic incident, the explicit memory system may be unavailable because the hippocampus is overwhelmed by stress hormones and therefore suppressed. Just which hormones cause the suppression is unclear. I have read studies that fault either adrenaline, noradrenaline, or cortisol, as well as studies that dispute the possibility that one or the other of these plays a role. At this time the sciences of memory and of PTSD are still quite young. Hopefully in the next decade or two this will become more clear.

Primarily it is the implicit memory system that is dominant both during a traumatic event and with regard to trauma recall, in part because it is unaffected by stress hormones. The amygdala, the limbic structure most involved in implicit memory, is also immune to stress hormones. So even when a person might not remember the explicit facts or progression of an event, it may be that there is plenty of implicit memory in body sensations and emotions. It is often the case with PTSD, and also in incidences of anxiety and panic, that something in the internal or external environment can trigger a slew of implicit memories without the cause being easily identified.

Part of phase I trauma treatment (see Chapter 7) can involve locating triggers in a survivor's daily life. Sometimes it helps just to identify them. At other times it will be necessary to make changes that directly dampen or neutralize the trigger or triggers.

Brett's and Jeffrey's Memories of Their Traumas
Both Brett and Jeffrey had major distortions in the memories of the events they had experienced. For the most part, Jeffrey had very little explicit memory of the explosion and its aftermath. However, he had

implicit memory of the event; there were many triggers. He was easily provoked by loud noises, particularly fireworks.

The recurrence of Brett's trauma 12 years after she was raped was provoked during a sexual interlude with her fiancé. It took some delving to discover the exact trigger, but once it became clear she was relieved. During that intimate occasion she had ended up in a physical position that was very similar to one she had been in during the rape. Her implicit memory had been activated by the proprioceptive sense, which (as you may recall from Chapter 4) is part of the interoceptive sensory nervous system. Proprioceptive triggering is rather common, though often unrecognized, in PTSD.

CHAPTER 6

Who Does and Does Not Get PTSD?

In general, it is estimated that as many as 90% of people around the world encounter trauma, per the DSM-IV-TR (APA, 2000) definition as experience that threatens life or bodily integrity, at some time in their lives (Frans, Rimma, Aberg, & Fredrikson, 2005). However, not all of those, not even a large portion, develop PTSD. The numbers may surprise you. As mentioned before, in actuality, only around 20% of those exposed to traumatic events will eventually develop PTSD (Elliott, 1997). However, as you might expect, rates among those who suffered at the hands of another human (assault, rape, torture, incest) are higher than among those struck by natural disasters (flood, earthquake) and accidents (falls, injuries).

For a long time it was assumed that it was the type of trauma that was encountered that would or would not make one vulnerable to PTSD. The first criteria, in the 1980 edition of the DSM-III (APA, 1980 p.238), stated that PTSD arose from incidents that "would evoke significant symptoms of distress in almost everyone." It was some years later before it was recognized that people respond differently to stress and traumatic events. Take, for example, the evidence by newsreel of the responses of the citizens of Haiti following the 2010 devastating earthquakes. Some of the people were in terror, others were angry, and a good number took advantage of the situation to loot, steal, and sell children. Conversely, the majority of the population calmly pitched in to help each other by sharing water and food, creating shelters and safety, and even raising the sense of community and optimism through singing in groups on the street. Now it is fairly well accepted that it is the individual's perception of and response to threat that will make the difference in whether or not someone is traumatized and eventually develops PTSD. In that way, trauma, to a large extent, is in the eye (and mind and body) of the beholder.

A recent example from someone close to me will help to illustrate this point. My 84-year-old friend, Howard, had his car stolen at knife-point recently. The police gave him a lift home. As soon as he got in, he called to tell me the tale. After I got past my brief disbelief (he can be quite the jokester), I settled into concern for him: No, he wasn't injured. All the thieves wanted was the car, so when he surrendered the keys they left him alone and just drove off. But of course I was also concerned for his emotional state: "Are you okay? Are you scared?" His reply floored me. "No, what good would that do?" "Weren't you scared?" I continued to probe. "No. That wouldn't do me any good. But I am mad!" And that was that. He was fine. As he said, he was (under-standably) angry. But he was not the least bit scared or anxious then or later. He believed the thieves only wanted the car, so he never felt his life was in danger. He agreed that it was a good idea to change the locks on his home (they had taken all of his keys), which we did before it got dark. But for him that was just a matter-of-fact precaution. He was not scared of a break-in.

Certainly I would have had a different emotional reaction to the same set of events, as I suppose a good portion of you reading this would also. Many people would experience fear for their lives, and some of those would develop PTSD under similar circumstances. But clearly, not everyone would. So if trauma is not a universal result of what we would objectively call a traumatic incident, how does that influence our theories and treatment? It begs the question: Faced with the same life-threatening incident, what distinguishes those who are not affected much at all, and those who are traumatized yet recover easily, from those who develop PTSD? The discussions below may throw some light on possible clues.

Peritraumatic Dissociation

To dissociate means to split consciousness in some way. Dissociative disorders, as discussed in Chapter 3, involve chronic splitting of some sort. Many people can experience one or more periods of dissociation without having a disorder. If you have found yourself arrived home with little or no memory of the drive, you have touched on a common, mild form of dissociation. The driving is so routine and everything you need to do is automatic, so your mind wanders somewhere else.

Dissociation during a traumatic event, peritraumatic dissociation, is very common. The consciousness splits, resulting in distortions of experience and memory. Following such an episode, people will describe that the passage of time slowed down, or that they did not feel any emotion or pain, or sometimes there is no memory of the occurrence at all. It is the timing of dissociation that happens during the traumatic event that continues to be a major predictive factor in who does and does not develop PTSD (Marshall & Schell, 2002; Ozer, Best, Lipsey, & Weiss, 2003).

There must be a relationship between the freeze response and dissociation, though this is not often discussed in the literature. Many who have frozen in response to threat describe much the same kinds of distortions as those who have dissociated. As a clinician, the difference between the one and the other is sometimes difficult to distinguish. Therefore, it may be possible that freezing during a traumatic incident may also predict PTSD, though I cannot find theoretical literature to support my hypothesis.

Taking a Trauma History

For the therapist, it is always a good idea to have a relatively complete case history on each client. For clients, having an idea of their own background can help to put the traumas they are dealing with into a greater context. Generally, knowing about early childhood resources and deficits will have a positive impact on both understanding and resolving later issues and traumas. In addition, having a list of the encountered traumatic incidents can help to put them into perspective and prioritize how and when to address each one.

However, there is an important tactic to factor in when either taking a client history or reviewing and writing up your own. To minimize launching the individual into hyperarousal or flashback, it is of utmost importance to compile the history without attention to detail. That is, just stick to the naming and listing of the traumatic incidents. Obtaining the necessary information while maintaining protective boundaries will help to ensure that the history taking is just that, only a collection of historical data and not a provocation of a flood of unmanageable trauma memories. In fact, sometimes it can be a very containing and calming exercise for traumatized people (with a therapist or on their own) to create such a list. It can be reassuring to see on paper that the difficulties of one's life have a very clear and legitimate source. In addition, writing down that kind of list can also make evident, with pen and paper, that the amount of trauma is finite rather than infinite. This is one type of containment that can make the goal of recovery more accessible. At the least, it will help both therapist and client to organize their view of and approach to trauma recovery.

Now, of course, it is tempting—often compelling—when naming a trauma to want to go further and either ask for more information (the therapist) or begin to recount some of the details (the client). This is exactly where patience, skill, and determination are all required. To protect the client from being overwhelmed, at this point it is necessary to hold back and stick with simply naming each trauma, for example:

- I was raped when I was 15.
- My grandfather, whom I was close to, suddenly died when I was 8.
- When I was 22 I had a serious car accident.

List no more than that for each one, even though it is so very tempting to want to know or say more. Maintaining this kind of restraint can be an exercise in containment for both client and therapist. Moreover, learning to merely name rather than detail a past trauma might be a critical first step in learning to control other, heretofore seemingly unmanageable, symptoms.

This brings up a very important issue for trauma therapists. It is vitally important that anyone working professionally with traumatized individuals be prepared to contain their curiosity (Rothschild, 2010b). It is critical that you cultivate and maintain the capacity to not know the details of what happened to one or perhaps many of your clients. You need to be able to continue to help them in the absence of detailed information. Lack of containment on the part of the professional will instead risk prematurely, sometimes totally inappropriately, propelling the client you mean to help straight into overwhelming dysregulation, flashback, or worse.

Something similar applies to friends and family of the traumatized. It may never be appropriate for them to know actual details because it may not be good for the survivor to reveal them. On the other hand, it could be hazardous to the loved ones themselves to hear the details; it could be traumatizing for them too. Remember, one of the DSM criteria for PTSD involves hearing about trauma that has befallen a loved one. There is another important concern: Telling the details of trauma to close relations could risk changing the interaction between some or all of them in a way that would not be helpful to their future relationship.

Resources

Another useful tactic for taking a trauma history—and, actually, for dealing with trauma altogether—is to pay a great deal of attention to resources (Rothschild, 2000). Resources, in this regard, are any of those factors that help someone cope with adversity, including the following:

- Practical things such as good locks on the doors and windows, a smoke alarm, adequate shelter and food, and so on.
- Abilities such as strength and agility, and activities like walking, sports, and weight training all contribute to physical resources.
- Personality traits and defense mechanisms are examples of psychological resources.
- Both humans and animals who are or were supportive, loving, protective, safe, and so on are vital resources whether the contact exists in the present or was realized in the past.
- Both religious and secular spiritual beliefs and practices, including connections to nature, provide tremendous comfort and reassurance to many.

One of the things that clearly distinguishes people who develop PTSD from those who do not is the amount and effectiveness of their resources, particularly support from humans, animals, and the spiritual realm. Years ago I was reminded of the power of simple human support when I met a young man who had been brutally assaulted as a teenager. After he outlined for me the circumstances and scenario, I would have expected the lad to have PTSD. But, in fact, he was doing just fine even though he had never had professional help. When I asked him what made the difference for him, he talked of two important factors. The first was his religion. The second was the dog he had at the time, who had stayed steadily by his side throughout the aftermath. Though he mourned the dog's passing a few years later, he still maintained the sense of her by his side. When times would get rocky in his current life, he would continue to call on both his religious faith and the memory of his beloved pet.

Stress Inoculation

Amazing as it may sound, trauma is not always a bad thing. Once resolved, either in the short or longterm, the results of trauma can sometimes serve to help an individual to be better able to manage both the small and large stresses of everyday life. In fact, it is speculated that one of the functions of the increased adrenaline output during a traumatic incident is to sear the memory of what happened deeply into the brain so that something similar might be avoided or better managed in the future.

We know from events such as the World Trade Center attacks of September 11, 2001, the Indian Ocean tsunami of December 2004, and the Haiti earthquake of February 2010 that trauma not only makes for victims but also for heroes. Of course, heroes are not immune to PTSD. On the other hand, the act of helping others often reduces the severity of the psychological consequences of trauma.

Do you know about curling? You may have seen it played during the Winter Olympics. It is that crazy sport where a heavy disc is slid down an icy path by one player while several others, using brooms, furiously sweep the ice ahead of the disc. The aim is to help the disc move—this way or that, faster or slower—to land at a desirable spot in the circular goal. Relatively recently a term was coined in Scandinavia (I have seen and heard its origin ascribed to both a Dane and a Swede) to describe parents who are (in essence) always sweeping the way smooth for their children. A curling parent would be one who attempts to minimize a child's stress, perhaps even intervening in conflicts or problems inappropriately or prematurely. The intention is to make the child's life as stress free as possible. Those who protect their children in this way believe that all stress is harmful. Another term for the same phenomenon is helicopter parent or hovering parent. Unfortunately, even though the intention is well meaning, many of these kids emerge from such families with less resilience than would otherwise be expected. It appears that preventing all conflict and stress diminishes the ability to develop tools and resources needed for coping with stress and adversity in healthy ways. So while the early protection seemed to help the children, in some ways it actually ended up handicapping a good portion of them. The resources they might have gained from having to deal with normal stresses have eluded them.

Attachment

Through the 1990s and into the new century, neuroscience caught up to psychotherapy and gave us a scientific understanding for many things we already knew either intuitively, through observation, or via common sense. Most obvious of these is the importance of our relationship with our mother or other primary caretakers in the first years of life and then through childhood. This relationship is crucial for, among other things, determining how we will later manage all sorts of adversity including stress and traumatic stress. The bonding of healthy attachment imbues resilience, affect tolerance and regulation, optimism, self-esteem, and so on. All of these traits are necessary to manage the ups and downs of life, including trauma. The more consistent and loving the early relationships, the easier it is for a person to face and conquer difficulties. That is not to say that a person who has the advantage of healthy attachment will be immune to PTSD. However, it does confer an advantage.

As logic would have it, the contrary situation also exists. When early attachment fails in one or more ways, the consequences can be felt through a lifetime. Those who are hurt, neglected, or even just miss out on consistent loving care in their early years may not develop the ability to easily spring back from difficulties throughout their lives.

It is, however, also possible to lose resilience. Even that which has been developed through good bonding can become compromised. Some traumas can be so massive and overwhelming that no matter how good a person's attachment and resources, PTSD still looms. But it is usual for those with the most secure early foundations to fare the best in the wake of trauma.

Gender Differences

There is a surprisingly small body of literature exploring the differences between males and females in their vulnerability and reactions to trauma. This is unfortunate as understanding these variations can vastly improve therapeutic treatment options as well as self-help approaches. Just the fact of understanding that men and boys, women and girls may have varying experiences and outcomes to similar events can be comforting to survivors who may be confused or feel ashamed that they did not respond as others did.

Though men and boys certainly suffer plenty of trauma, the research consistently shows higher rates for both trauma exposure and development of PTSD in women and girls. The reasons for this disparity appear related to females being much more vulnerable to sexual abuse and incest. Though males can also be sexually victimized, the frequency is significantly less. Men and boys are more likely to encounter trauma through other acts of violence, accidents, and military service (Breslau, 2002; Tolin & Foa, 2002).

Following on the above discussion on peritraumatic dissociation, Allan Schore (2002) and Bruce Perry (1996), among other specialists in neuropsychology, observed that while men are more likely to react to trauma with flight and fight survival responses, women and children are more apt to dissociate or freeze. This in itself may account for much of the greater likelihood for females to develop PTSD.

Cultural Differences

Culture has a huge influence on reactions and responses to as well as recovery from trauma and the development of PTSD. This is often neglected in research, literature, and practice, most of which is weighted toward the "first world," particularly the United States and Western Europe. Ethan Watters (2010), in his provocative book Crazy Like Us: The Globalization of the American Psyche, argued that the Western world is imposing its view of psychopathology, including PTSD, onto the third world with sometimes disastrous impact. Many of his points have merit as trauma studies and treatments are developed primarily in the United States and Europe. Interventions tend to be universally applied, for example in Asia or Africa, without evaluating or adjusting their potential relevance in those cultures. The result, Watters wrote, can lead to a loss of culturally innate resources for managing trauma that might otherwise make professional intervention unnecessary. He observed that in some cases, the culture ends up in worse shape than if there had been no intervention from Western practitioners.

I tend to agree with Watters's viewpoint as I have shared some of his observations and concerns for a long time. On a limited basis, I have been able to make some inroads along these lines while providing probono consultation to therapists working with trauma in third world countries. The needs in many of those places are very different. It is clear that many of the tools we have developed for use in the West do not work well or are in conflict with cultural norms or beliefs. It is critical to remember that both first and third world cultures managed long before the emergence of psychotherapy or trauma specialists. For me this is a humbling fact: People survived trauma before me, my methods, and my books, and will after I am gone. In many cultures, it is their traditions of cohesion, support, and community that are the keys to trauma recovery. Supporting the ways in which a culture already helps and heals its members will be central in making a meaningful contribution to trauma healing that is relevant and compatible with a particular way of life. That would be much preferable to imposing possibly unwelcome, even potentially damaging, alien philosophies and methods.

For example, Zoee, a trauma volunteer in a large third world country, shared her frustration with me that she could not use the tools she had arrived with to help the people in the village she had been assigned to. Their own ways of coping with trauma were to joke about it and then to tell each other to forget about it and be strong. They would assure one another that they would manage. The therapist wanted to help them to contact their deeper emotions and talk about the traumas they had experienced. Instead, I advised that she ask the natives to teach her their ways first. After developing some contact and trust, she then might ask them about where, in their culture, there was a place (if any) for emotions. In that way she could introduce the idea with respect for their traditional coping mechanisms. And if there was no place for her version of emotional expression, she would have to back off that idea. What emerged was an exciting exploration into the role of movement, music, and dance in soothing upsets and healing trauma in that culture.

But paying attention to cultural differences is not just relevant in other countries. It is vitally important within the offices, agencies, and institutions that help trauma victims anywhere in the world. Just because the help being offered takes place in a particular country does not mean that all those seeking help will be residents of that country or adherents to that culture. Even within a cohesive community there can be huge differences in culture from one neighborhood, block, or family to the next.

One of the best things trauma therapists can do (or for that matter, any psychotherapist) is to ask their clients to teach them about their culture. This can include regular discussions on the pros and cons of various interventions in light of a client's cultural background as well as each one's individual needs.

I am tremendously aware of this dilemma when writing my books. All of them are written toward a primarily Western readership. One of the ways I compensate for possible cultural discrepancies is by repeatedly emphasizing the importance of regarding individual differences. That is the only way I know of to ensure you will be able to recognize and respect cultural, religious, or any other kinds of differences that could enhance or interfere with treatment outcome.

Which Factors Contributed to Brett's and Jeffrey's Vulnerability to PTSD?

For Jeffrey, PTSD was a strong likelihood in the wake of his traumatic experiences. In a way he was preprogrammed for it. He came from an unstable home with an alcoholic and violent father. His chronically ill mother had died only a year prior to his enlisting in the army. Though he had good friends, those bonds could not make up for the ones he missed in early childhood. In addition, the trauma he encountered was terribly gruesome and occurred very early in his military career. He had not had time to develop a thicker skin for at least some of the kinds of distressing incidents a soldier will likely be faced with.

Brett's picture is different. Her early childhood was very secure and she had a good bond with her parents. It is partly for that reason that the depth of her trauma was not evident for 12 years. Everyone assumed that the support of friends and family had been sufficient. When she emerged with PTSD those many years later, for a while she was at a loss to understand why. Gradually it became apparent to both herself and her therapist that what had looked like resolution in the aftermath of the rape had only been remission. Her parents had been greatly upset by their daughter's rape and Brett had been in a hurry to get better to save them further suffering. What had looked like a cure was really her attempts to put away a large portion of her upset. Sometimes this kind of dissociation or repression can successfully last a lifetime. But in Brett's case it did not. In the end it was the love she shared with her parents that both helped her initially and later underlay her development of PTSD.

Moreover, Brett froze during the rape, which is very typical. Like most victims of rape, she was unable to fight back. Jeffrey dissociated when the landmine exploded. He describes his memory of the scenario as having the feel of a very, very bad hallucinogenic trip. Both of them suffered a large amount of shame because of their inability to react at the time of their incidents (see Chapter 13 for the role of shame in trauma and trauma healing).

Treating PTSD

Treatment for trauma and PTSD has evolved significantly over the last century, accelerating through the last decade of the twentieth and the first decade of the twenty-first centuries. Currently there are dozens of options for the trauma survivor—each and every one with its own set of controversies. Following chapters address the various options in the psychotherapy realm, including the cognitive therapies, somatic psychotherapies, energy therapies, and applications from more traditional psychotherapies such as psychoanalysis and psychodynamic approaches (Chapter 8), psychiatry, which primarily treats with prescription medication (Chapter 9); mindfulness and meditation, which have been rediscovered in psychotherapy particularly with application to trauma treatment (Chapter 10); and somatic methods that might be useful adjuncts such as yoga (Chapter 11). However, before paying attention to specific interventions, it is important to address some basic issues that are pertinent to every course of trauma therapy.

Phased Treatment: The Gold Standard for Structuring Trauma Therapy

In the late 1800s and early 1900s, Pierre Janet was specializing in the study and treatment of hysteria and trauma. In many ways he may be thought of as the father of modern trauma therapy. His insights laid the foundation for much of trauma therapy as it is now practiced. Most importantly for modern therapies, Janet identified a logical structure for working with hysteria and trauma that continues to be an extremely important foundation today. He identified that trauma healing required a three-phase approach (Janet, 1898, 1919):

- Phase I: Stabilization and safety
- Phase II: Remembering and processing trauma memories
- Phase III: Integration with family and culture, and normal daily life

Each step plays an integral role in trauma treatment.

Phase I: Stabilization and Safety

In the first stage, the emphasis is on helping trauma survivors to gain control over their symptoms. This is necessary to ensure that the circumstances of an individual's daily life are safe and secure, and that the therapeutic environment and relationship are (and are perceived as) safe. Overstatement of the importance of this step is not possible; it is vital if trauma recovery is to be realized. Making the time investment to achieve these goals of stabilization and safety will be well rewarded. To shortchange this stage can lead to unnecessary problems and risks in the subsequent stages, especially phase II (discussed below). Many clients and therapists are in such a hurry to get to the work of phase II that they shortchange phase I or skip it altogether. That can be a fundamental error. Without first establishing stabilization and safety, the work of phases II and III may become impossible or require much more time than would otherwise have been necessary. There are those who mistakenly disregard phase I as not being a legitimate part of trauma therapy or treatment per se because the focus is not on the traumatic incidents. However, successful accomplishment of this stage is a critical step, perhaps the most critical, in trauma recovery. It is a central part of trauma treatment, at least equal to the relevance of phase II.

This book's preface put forward the most important goal for trauma treatment: Improve the quality of life of the trauma survivor. That goal is also consistent with the stabilization and safety goals of phase I. For most trauma survivors, gaining mastery over their symptoms and securing their environments will greatly improve their life quality.

For some survivors, accomplishing phase I requires little time. Individuals of this sort are usually fairly resilient. They have their home lives as well as family and friend networks already in place, ready to support their needs. For this type of person, phase I may only last one or two sessions.

However, there are a good many traumatized individuals whose lack of resilience and support system indicate that meeting the goals of phase I may take a long time, perhaps even years. In fact, for a portion of trauma survivors, the best trauma therapy will be restricted, for the most part, to phase I. Some may, in reality, never be ready for phase II. It will be important to identify those who belong to this group of clients, as moving on to phase II with someone not adequately equipped from a successful phase I could have dire consequences. Sticking with phase I when necessary can demand a good deal of patience from both therapist and client. The pull of delving into trauma memory can be strong. It is at this point that the survivor needs to learn to contain the need to find out or tell every detail of what happened and for the therapist to contain her curiosity about it (Rothschild, 2010b). In some cases, the safest course for the survivor will be to steer away from phase II altogether (see below). In that event, client and therapist must be in a position to accept this graciously to avert potential disaster.

Phase I treatment involves increasing anything that improves the client's life and ability to cope. Some of the areas of focus will be affect tolerance, grounding, functioning on a daily basis, resources, networks of both friends and family members, exercise, the therapeutic relationship, and so on.

Phase II: Remembering and Processing Trauma Memories

Phase II involves the processing of trauma memories. Work in this phase is vital to the recovery of a good portion of trauma survivors. However, it will not be indicated or even helpful for another portion of survivors. Below, I spend a good bit of space discussing why and when to bypass phase II. That is because many practitioners and clients are not aware there is any option for or reason to avoid detailing trauma memories. The work of phase II is already generally accepted in the field of trauma treatment. So here I would like to make a case for an additional option for our clients: to not work with their memories at all.

Phase II is the usual emphasis in the professional and self-help literature and at trauma workshops and training. Most discussions focus on varying ways to process trauma memories. Few spend much (if any) time recognizing that portion of survivors for whom processing trauma will seriously compromise their ability to function on a daily basis. For them, persisting with the challenges of phase I will be most appropriate. It may help to understand how phase II, opening up the past—what one would assume to be a helpful step—could potentially be hurtful.

Surviving psychological trauma involves the development of defenses that are necessary to continue on, to cope, despite what happened. Many trauma survivors have well-established defenses for coping. Actually, that is exactly what defenses are, coping strategies. To be able to process one's trauma memories, to look at the past in detail, those defenses must, necessarily, loosen up. Loosening defenses is always destabilizing, at least somewhat, as the resources for coping that accompany them also become more slack.

People who are basically stable to begin with, or who have become reliably stable through phase I work, are usually able to tolerate these consequential doses of instability. They typically recover their stability quickly at each step along the way. In those instances, the resolving of trauma memories has the potential to enhance resilience and the ability to function. However, for those who are unstable and have not adequately managed phase I, the processing of trauma memories will only increase their instability. The result will be that they have even less to hold onto than they did before they began processing their memories. For this group of individuals, it is not a good idea to work in phase II, at least until they have really succeeded in phase I.

Therapists who consult with me often raise concerns about clients who chronically dissociate, decompensate, or seem to be taking a very long time when working with trauma memories. When we review such situations, we regularly find that phase I has either been skipped or shortchanged, or that a client who successfully accomplished phase I has somehow slipped back into instability. In all of these instances, shifting focus to phase I, at least for a few sessions, makes eventual continuation of phase II much easier. It is possible to pay attention to this when using any model or method for phase II. Any one of them can be interrupted along the way, if the survivor is not coping well. In fact, reclaiming a firm foundation of stability from a revisit to phase I, will make eventual return to phase II work more secure. It will also, generally, make it possible for the therapy to wrap up more quickly.

A second, but often unrecognized, group who should always bypass phase II are those who, for whatever reason, do not want to look backward and revisit their past. To some readers it may seem obvious and unnecessary to mention this. However, there are countless books and therapies that advocate for processing memories no matter what. I hope that if you are one who believes memories must always be reviewed, you will consider this: Forcing someone to remember the horrors of trauma may be as, if not sometimes more, traumatizing than the original event itself. Please never push or force yourself, your friend or family member, or your client into facing trauma memories against their wishes.

There is a prevailing belief in the trauma recovery world that all traumas need to be resolved (memories processed) for a person to be well, cured, healed, or whatever. But that is really not the case. At the professional lectures and trainings I give around the world, I now routinely ask this question: "How many of you have a trauma in your history that you have not worked on but nonetheless function fairly well in spite of?" Amazingly, half to two thirds of the audiences raise their hands. I take this unscientific poll to emphasize the truth that most of us, to some extent, live relatively well with unresolved trauma. In the face of that fact, it makes no sense to force anyone to face the past against their will and without the promise that it will facilitate a better quality of life for them.

Phase III: Integration With Family and Culture, and Normal Daily Life

Janet recommended that phase III, integration, be the culmination of trauma therapy. However, a good case can be made for actually distributing focus on integration throughout work with both phases I and II. That way integration is in motion with and a vital partner of every step of a trauma recovery process. This is a much better strategy for integration than waiting until the end of trauma memory processing. In general, the best therapy and self-help of any sort involves integration of each resolution, new resource, insight, and so on into daily life as soon as it is realized. That way the new tools can be used immediately, and life improves step by step, not just at the end of the process.

Most trauma therapy looks backward, that is, to phase II and the processing of the memories of one or more traumatic events. As discussed above, processing what happened in the past can be helpful for a good portion of trauma survivors. However, putting the spotlight on what happened then is only really useful if what is learned can be applied to the present, to a person's daily life. So for any trauma therapy to be successful, integration—in both phase I and phase II—

must build bridges to relevant points in the current life of the survivor. For example, if one of the trauma elements was being isolated, being unable to talk with anyone, a major integrative step might be helping the client to talk with selected friends and family members about what happened. In another instance, for someone working with phase I, increasing mindfulness of body sensations may help to anticipate and better manage current potentially stressful situations.

The general bottom line is that what most matters in life is what is happening now. So trauma therapy must always keep ties with and relevance to the here and now even when the pull to wallow in the past is strong.

Short Versus Long-Term Trauma Therapy

The question of the length of therapy is relevant for therapists and current or potential clients. There are at least three areas to address in this debate. The first has to do with the practicalities of third-party payment and nonprofit agencies. The second is about the claims of a handful of trauma therapy programs that they can cure or heal trauma within a few sessions. The third focuses on evaluating individual needs.

Who Pays?

Whether clients choose short or long-term treatment will, in part, depend on what they can afford. Currently in the United States and many other countries, insurance companies and public health programs (such as the National Health Service in the United Kingdom) severely limit the number of therapy sessions they will permit and pay for. Frankly, these limitations are about money and nothing else. They have nothing to do with client needs or quality of service. This makes sense, though. Of course these organizations and agencies want to conserve their funds; restricting the number of paid hours helps to balance their budgets, pay their employees and executives, and meet other expenses. The clients who have adequate resources have the luxury of choosing whether to go outside of these systems and pay privately for as many sessions as they want or need. However, those who are dependent on the public or nonprofit sector will not have so many options.

It is an unfortunate trend. Just as insurance company executives are now telling our doctors which medications they can prescribe and which treatments they can apply, it is a genuine shame that they are also telling psychotherapists of all types to hurry up processes, even (and especially) those that might need more time. Unfortunately for some of our clients, this means not getting what they need. In the worst-case scenarios, clients end up worse than before they started because traumatic material is provoked without adequate time to address the fallout. There is a good deal of pressure on practitioners to jump to phase II work, that is, addressing the trauma memories. Attention to stabilization and the client's quality of life gets lost too often. Sometimes that results in clients being pushed into facing issues they are ill prepared for. This does not make much sense and sometimes can end up being all the more expensive as some of these clients will need further care, even hospitalization.

These policies also place unfair pressure on practitioners. In my training programs, I regularly hear complaints from therapists who feel forced to go against their own best judgment to comply with the rules of the workplace or third-party payer. I have known many colleagues who suffer greater compassion fatigue due to these pressures. They become torn. They must abide by the limitations of their payers but are often aware of compromising treatment quality. It is a critical dilemma.

When a course of trauma therapy is drastically limited by funding constraints, it is most advisable to stick to phase I treatment. Do not forget that our first obligation is to not do harm. Increasing stability and improving quality of life, laying aside trauma memory focus until there is adequate time to do it justice, will much better serve our clients in these situations.

Can Therapy Really Be That Quick?

The proponents of several trauma therapy methods claim that these methods will resolve trauma memories in five or fewer sessions. Though this is possible in some instances, unfortunately, such advertising does not usually include discussion of limitations. Short-term therapy success with phase II is only possible with a single, uncomplicated trauma in a person who is relatively stable to begin with. When paired with the right therapy and therapist, some of these clients are able to move through their memories quickly. However, this is the exception and not the norm. Most clients need a reasonable amount of attention to phase I before they are prepared to address their memories. And phase II memory processing requires time to be addressed responsibly.

There are a good many clients for whom phase I will be the whole trauma therapy—the ones who are the most unstable and often come from backgrounds that include very early neglect, abandonment, or abuse. Therapies with these individuals need to include attention to attachment issues and the therapeutic relationship. In that case, five sessions will not begin to be adequate.

So, as with most everything else, the time a trauma therapy takes is very idividual. It proceeds best when there is the option to have as many or as few sessions as are needed. It would be a relief for many practitioners and clients if the insurance companies would return the power to make professional treatment decisions (in medicine, psychotherapy, and so on) to the professionals who are trained to make those decisions themselves. I hope that day comes soon.

Evaluating Individual Needs

The real key to successful trauma therapy is evaluating and meeting individual needs. For some clients, this will mean only a few sessions with little or no focus on the therapeutic relationship, only a short time in phase I and a few sessions for phase II. For others it may be years, every bit of the time spent in phase I with the therapeutic relationship serving as the main vehicle of the therapy. Most clients, however, will fit somewhere in between.

Predicting what a client might need is not easy, and we have few guidelines in the trauma field. Probably the diagnostic tools most relevant to trauma therapy are those which measure dissociation. The Dissociative Experiences Scale appears to be the most popular. However, you do not always need an instrument to evaluate dissociative potential, as often clients will tell you or it will be obvious from interacting with and observing them. No matter how you make this assessment, doing so will help you to estimate therapy length and which phase to focus on. Dissociative clients tend to be more fragile and need more careful attention to establishing stability as well as a greater emphasis on the therapeutic relationship.

The number of unresolved traumas in the client's history and how the client talks about them can also provide a guideline. Those with multiple traumas who speak of them in an overwhelmed and confused manner, often obsessively, will also need more time and attention to phase I. The ones who can speak about one trauma at a time without being overwhelmed or overlapping them will likely be more stable and therefore better candidates for eventual phase II work. Such stable clients will probably require fewer total sessions.

When there are complicating concurrent conditions such as bipolar, character or dissociative disorders, substance abuse, and so on, making and prioritizing treatment steps will necessarily be more difficult and time consuming.

Does the Therapeutic Relationship Matter?

The short answer is yes, of course. We have always known this. Even with the advent of specialized treatment methods, the therapeutic relationship continues to associate most consistently with therapy outcome (Lambert & Barley, 2001). However, how much it matters will depend on individual factors. Contact and support of all types (also from the therapist) are well-recognized mediators of stress following traumatic events. That appears to be true whether the contact and support are immediate or come later on. Therefore, the therapeutic relationship figures in no matter if it is initiated soon or long after the initial trauma. So just the fact of a warm, empathetic, supportive other is helpful. Of course more may be needed, but never underestimate the value of caring contact, also from the helping professional.

So, for all traumatized clients, the relationship will be important, although it is those clients who are the most fragile, dissociated, and overwhelmed for whom the relationship will matter most. These clients have lacked secure attachment throughout their lives, usually beginning in early childhood. For them the relationship with the therapist may be the most important dimension of the therapy. Particularly for trauma clients who have concurrent diagnoses of borderline personality disorder and attachment disorder, the therapeutic relationship may be much more vital than any therapy method or model.

This is a frequent consultation and supervision issue. Therapists routinely complain about clients who come week after week without appearing to make any visible progress. The practitioners often feel guilty that they are not doing enough or frustrated that the client is inert. Time and again, all it takes is some simple probing on my part to reveal the glue that is holding the client in the therapy: the supportive relationship. In many cases, a wealth of big and small changes are happening below the visible surface as the client slowly absorbs the consistent presence of this interested and caring other. Obviously such a pace and focus would not be satisfactory therapy for every trauma client. But for numerous clients, such steady presence is exactly what they need.

What Is Evidence-Based Treatment?

Many therapists will be familiar with this term, but for those who are not and for the client readers, a discussion of evidence-based treatment may be useful.

Evidence-based practice in psychotherapy is adapted from the concept of evidence-based medicine. It has long been vital in medicine to test and retest both medications and procedures under recognized methods to distinguish those which are helpful and do as claimed from those which are not and do not. Standardized scientific research has been applied for these investigations. Into the 20th century, the idea of evidence-based treatment broadened to include other areas of treatment, most notably psychotherapy and, eventually, trauma therapy.

Those who adhere to evidence-based practice apply only those methods and theories which have a body of peer-reviewed research to support their claims. In principle this is a wonderful concept, but it needs to be taken with a grain of salt. Psychotherapy is not medicine and the human psyche has many, many variables. Judging therapy research results is neither the same, nor as straightforward, as identifying whether or not a bacterial throat infection is quickly cured by this or that antibiotic. People are just not so easily described by those types of objective variables.

The main difficulty here is that research on trauma therapy methods is all outcome research. That means there is some kind of testing before and after the therapy in an attempt to measure that method's effectiveness. Unfortunately, outcome research has more bias than just about any other kind of research. This research limitation is expanded on in chapter 8.

Many insurance companies, agencies, employee assistance programs, and other third-party payers now only accept therapies that have outcome studies evaluating their effectiveness. They believe that only models with a research backing can be used successfully. It is an understandable position, if unfortunate and sometimes misleading. Limiting available options to only those in the research base can cheat clients of help that might better suit their individual needs.

Even when the evidence demonstrates something is effective, it cannot be generalized to conclude it will be effective with everyone. In fact, that would never be the case. Two analogies might help. First, take penicillin. No doubt it is a wonder drug. A huge base of evidence supports this belief. However, there is also a large population for whom it is harmful, even lethal. So just because the evidence base shows it to be of benefit, does not mean—in any way—that it will help everyone. For the second analogy, consider antidepressant drugs. Even the ones that are approved for use and are hailed for their demonstrated success, help only a fraction of depressed people. A highly comprehensive study of 65,000 people on antidepressant drugs reported in the American Journal of Psychiatry showed that success rates for individual medications ranged from only 30% to 50% (Simon, Savarino, Operskalski, & Wang, 2006). In fact, one of the difficulties in prescribing such medications is that it may take several tries before one that works for a specific individual is found. Thankfully, there are many to choose from.

Truth be told, this is also the case for trauma therapy. Evidence of effectiveness for a particular method is no guarantee it will be effective for a particular client. Therefore, as with the antidepressants, it is best when a selection of options are available for sampling. A good number of therapies do not have scientific research, but have anecdotal evidence that they could be useful for some people. Bottom line? The best expert on what is effective for an individual is that individual. A good recommendation is to offer options to clients and let them choose the one or ones that appeal to them. Then you can proceed to test out one or the other. If you get a good result, continue. If you get an adverse result, try something else. See Chapter 12, "How to Tell if a Treatment Works," for more on evaluating therapy.

Group Therapy for Trauma: Caution

Getting adequate support and contact is always important for trauma recovery. And groups for trauma survivors have been popular since the beginning of organized trauma treatment in the 1980s. One of the features of PTSD is isolation. Trauma survivors feel terribly alone with whatever it was that happened to them. Finding others who have experienced similar incidents is an idea that is very appealing to many, and actually quite logical. Who can better understand what you are going through than those who have been there themselves? So on the surface, the idea of group therapy for trauma looks like a good one. And sometimes it is. However, sometimes it is not. Many trauma groups, particularly for those who have been physically and sexually abused, often become more traumatizing than supportive. Shop carefully if you or your client wants to be in a group. Look for one with an emphasis on building support and daily life skills.

Traditionally, traumatized people have come together in groups, either self-help support groups or group therapy, and told their trauma stories to each other. Unfortunately, this has not proven to be a very good idea. Often they end up traumatizing each other. People with PTSD are just too vulnerable to having their own trauma memories and symptoms provoked—we often call this triggering. Moreover, when hearing the details of another's trauma, it can be difficult even for someone who has never experienced trauma to listen. But someone with PTSD may have limited tools for separating the other person's trauma from his own. The result can be increased distress, flashbacks, decompensation, and so on.

Successful trauma groups tend to keep the focus away from trauma stories, instead better equipping the members with tools for daily living and improving quality of life. The groups that teach survivors how to support each other without traumatizing each other are particularly valuable. Dialectical behavior therapy (see chapter 8) is particularly useful in this regard.

Current Methods of Trauma Therapy

The leading and most volatile controversy in the field of traumatic stress involves determining which methods of treatment are accepted by the mainstream and which are not. Choosing methods and evaluating their success continues to be a very stressful and confusing dilemma for practitioners as well as consumers. In general, the choice of a therapeutic method should be a matter of the taste and style of both therapist and client. Still, both therapists and clients continue to be forced to employ ill-fitting methods because of strict adherence to the evidence base by many organizations and individuals. Published outcome studies and statistics can be misleading and may or may not represent results one can actually count on in the therapy room with a particular individual. The bottom line is that no matter what is stated in print, no method appeals to or even comes close to working for everyone. In addition, many methods that have yet to amass research may still have plenty to offer a good number of people and should not be dismissed out of hand. In general, therapists should be skeptical of statistical reports that narrow educational and training options and clients should be skeptical of providers who exclusively adhere to only one or two ways of working.

A few years ago at a small professional seminar, the lecturer was discussing a fairly new treatment model that was rapidly growing in popularity (I will not name it here as there really are several models that could fit appropriately into this story). Though he was a proponent of the method, touting its many advantages, he was nonetheless evenhanded in his overview. As a part of his presentation, he also discussed potential difficulties one might encounter with that method, suggesting other methods that might better deal with those particular complications. During this part of the presentation, a rather distressed practitioner interrupted, asserting, "Well I use [that method] exclusively, and I never have any of those problems." That comment sums up the risks for single model use in a nutshell. The protesting therapist would likely never see those problems because she had nowhere else to go if they appeared. With her options so limited, she could not afford to consider that her favored method might have flaws that might need to be compensated for with a different method outside the realm of her expertise. Such is this type of treatment exclusivity. All too often I have heard other single-method therapists actually blame their client for a treatment failure, citing noncompliance or resistance. These practitioners never consider the possibility that the cause of the therapeutic failure may be that the method they are using may just not be suitable for that client. When the therapist has only one method to use, it is difficult to be able to acknowledge that some problems may actually lie in the method and not the client.

Therapists who train in, and have available for use, a variety of treatment choices for trauma therapy are the best pick for traumatized clients. Adherence to only one model means that there will not be another option if that particular model fails or is not a good fit for the client. Of course, each professional should train in only those methods that suit her own beliefs and style, but having several available will increase flexibility and, thereby, safety and ultimate success.

Remember, traumatized individuals need to increase mastery over their symptoms and their lives. This includes having a say in their therapy. A therapist whose basic stance is "my way or the highway" is not in a position to help clients gain self-control and learn to make good choices, as there is no choice in such a circumstance except to stay or to leave.

Choosing Methods: How to Interpret the Research
There is a marvelous little book first published in 1954 and still in print that anyone interested in research should take the time to read. It will only take you about 2 hours, as it is less than 150 pages in big type and has plenty of useful illustrations. The book is How to Lie With Statistics

by Darrell Huff. It was required reading for my very first psychology course and I have silently thanked that instructor many, many times over the past 40 years for assigning it. With tongue in cheek and plenty of solid information, this little volume will not only entertain you, it will also help you to be a much more savvy consumer and interpreter of research findings.

Research Bias

Below, I outline and discuss the most readily available models for treating PTSD. Some have research outcome studies that aim to evaluate effectiveness; others do not. In a way, it actually does not matter as it is ultimately the therapist and client who must decide which methods are helpful and which are not. Moreover, it is important to note that, unfortunately, outcome research has several weaknesses that call into question the value of results.

First, all research has bias. It is unavoidable. For example, companies that manufacture medication test and retest each one for effectiveness and safety. At the same time, of course they want to be successful and sell their products. The consequences of their inevitable research bias are publicly evident on an all-too-regular basis. How often do you read in the newspaper of wonder drugs and fantastic treatments that are enthusiastically introduced into the marketplace and then, months or years later, are withdrawn for failing to do as promised or, worse, causing actual harm?

In the trauma arena, organizations that use particular methods have a high investment—both professional and economic—in proving their success. Therefore, studies conducted by method proponents will tend to have a positive bias and those conducted by opponents will tend to have a negative bias. It is probably this phenomenon that underlies the confusion of research results I discovered a few years ago when looking at the outcome results of a popular method of trauma therapy. After looking at the then-available results, I made a tally for those studies that showed the method to be:

1. More effective than the comparison method or waitlist
2. Less effective than the comparison method or waitlist
3. Showed no effective difference to the comparison method or waitlist

The result was exactly the same number of tick marks in every tally column. I will not name which method I was looking at, as it does not matter. I have looked more and less informally at results for other methods and the end result is basically the same. The studies conducted by proponents demonstrate success; those conducted by opponents demonstrate failure; and the majority of the few genuinely independent studies tend to show no conclusive difference.

Research Subjects

Another area that calls the usefulness of trauma therapy outcome research into question is the samples of subjects that are used for the studies. Every published research study will tell you who the subjects are, but they will not always tell you who they barred from the study. In actuality, for every study many candidates are dismissed because they do not fit the study's parameters. Remember, outcome research is usually conducted to show that a particular method is useful, that it works for the population it is designed for. Therefore, people who will obviously not benefit from a method will be eliminated from a study. In the vast majority of trauma method outcome studies, subjects are not random—they are carefully chosen. In general, acceptable subjects will be relatively stable and have only a single trauma that is troubling them. People with multiple traumas, especially with complex issues or complicating personality disorders, are rarely accepted in outcome studies. This is not such a problem if you want to apply the research findings to work with stable clients who only have single or simple traumas. However, a large proportion (perhaps even a majority) of those seeking trauma therapy have multiple unresolved traumas and are not particularly or even at all stable. For such individuals, outcome research findings are virtually useless as all too little of it has been conducted with a truly random population. However, time and again, it is this same research that is quoted in designating which methods should be applied across the board to all clients within a clinic, institute, private practice, or insurance program.

How to Determine Success

So, who knows if a method is actually successful? Ultimately, it is the client. It is the person who suffers from trauma who will know whether or not a method or intervention is useful. See Chapter 12 for guidelines in making these evaluations.

Treatment Focus

As mentioned in Chapter 2, a disturbance of normal memory is the core of PTSD. So, understandably, the common wisdom for trauma therapy has always been to target and process those disturbed memories of the trauma. The belief is that by repeatedly reviewing what happened, the distress of the memory will diminish. Habituation and new ways of thinking about the event are the usual goals. Most models of trauma therapy adhere to this practice in one way or another. Some work with the entire memory all at once (e.g., prolonged exposure, traumatic incident reduction), and others break it down into bits (e.g., EMDR, somatic experiencing). However, it is rare for method trainers to suggest other options, that is, not processing memories completely or even at all. Such choices are critically important to include because, as discussed previously, memory processing can have negative consequences for some clients and there will be others who do not want to revisit their memories. Remember: a traumatized individual should never be forced to remember the horrors of her trauma in therapy. For many that would be tantamount to retraumatization. Of course there are situations in which a review of trauma memories is required, particularly when legal proceedings are involved or when a refugee is seeking asylum. However, in the course of trauma therapy, it should always be an option, not a necessity.

There is no reason that anyone should ever be required to do anything in trauma therapy—or any therapy for that matter—that they oppose.

I am often asked if such a refusal is avoidance. The question's implication is that the evasion of trauma memories is equivalent to doing something wrong. I could not disagree more strongly. In fact, it is a common way that individuals manage trauma on their own. Many people manage and recover from trauma without rehashing their memories over and over. Therefore, why should that not also be a valid option in trauma therapy?

Last, remember that trauma does not happen when people are in control of the circumstances. If they can stop the earthquake, prevent the death of a loved one, not be at the wrong place at the wrong time, there is no trauma. Every single trauma client has experienced an extreme instance of being out of control. For many reasons, including this, it makes no sense to take control of clients by forcing them to face previous terror. Allowing them the control to choose to not remember could be an essential step in recovery for some clients. The example below serves to illustrate one possibility.

Lisa, a client of mine during the time I lived in Denmark, was unable to swim or even go into a pool, lake, or the ocean. Her fear was so intense that she would pale and shiver just at the thought of expanses of water. She was not even able to get into a boat. She had nearly drowned when she was 3 when she fell, unobserved, into the lake by her family's summer house. Luckily the family dog had noticed and raised a ruckus barking until her father ran down to quiet him and discovered his little daughter flailing in the water.

At the time she first saw me, Lisa was 32 and expecting her first child. Knowing how much a parent influences a child, she was worried that her fear of water could easily be transferred to her daughter. Up until this point she had avoided talking to anyone about her dilemma because she assumed she would be required to remember the near drowning, something she was terrified to do. She came to me hoping I could help her with her fear of water without it being necessary to revisit her past.

We spent some sessions working with phase I, making sure of Lisa's general stability. She was somewhat fragile emotionally. Even if she had wanted to process her memories of drowning, I am not sure I would have agreed, at least in the first weeks that we worked together. Nonetheless, gradually she became more stable. Then I suggested that we could address her water fears directly without having to look at the past. Drawing on the cognitive-behavioral techniques of desensitization, we mapped out a plan to very gradually expose Lisa to greater amounts and depths of water. We both realized this could take many months, perhaps even a couple of years. But it was Lisa's preferred way to manage it. Moving slowly from small doses of imagining water to eventually sticking her toe in a pool, little by little we increased her tolerance of being in water. For Lisa, every step was a new victory. By the time her baby was born, she was able to be in a small pool or large hot tub. Continuing on after the birth, eventually Lisa could sit by the lake or ocean with her legs dangling in the water, feeling calm and comfortable. At this point Lisa decided to stop, feeling she had accomplished enough. She wanted to be able to take her daughter into a pool, but not into a lake or the ocean. Satisfied and relieved, Lisa said goodbye and went on to raise a daughter who never feared water.

Reviewing Available Trauma Therapy Methods

Practitioners of some of the methods below will insist on processing trauma memories. Others may also work well with people who are not candidates for that kind of work. For those clients who do want to process their memories and can manage without degrading their quality of life or decompensation, there are many good methods, though, as previously discussed, only a few have research studies to support their claims. Therapists and clients can evaluate usefulness in individual circumstances together (see Chapter 12).

All of the trauma therapies available today have roots in models that came before them. Where possible, I will (to the best of available knowledge) sketch the major influences of a particular model to put it into perspective with the others. Further, understanding the roots of various methods may help both therapist and client to better choose the ones to attempt and distinguish them from those which do not appeal or seem unsuitable for their situation.

Due to many factors, it is not possible to discuss (or even know about) every single therapy method that can be used to treat PTSD. Below are the ones that are most readily visible in my sphere.

Cognitive Therapies

In general, the cognitive therapies aim to help people with all sorts of emotional problems by identifying and then changing dysfunctional patterns of thought, feelings, and actions. The range of cognitive therapies has expanded significantly since first conceived by Aaron Beck in the mid-20th century. He first applied his ideas to helping depression, and then more generally. Around the same time, Albert Ellis was developing rational emotive therapy. Modern cognitive therapies, including those designed for helping trauma, are rooted in the early theories and methods of these two men.

Cognitive therapies will appeal to those therapists and clients who prefer a more practical and matter-of-fact approach. The emphasis is usually weighted toward the internal thought and emotional processes of the clients more than the relationship between therapist and client (though of course there are exceptions). The core of cognitive theory proposes that what we think shapes how we feel and behave. The therapy method involves correcting unhelpful and dysfunctional thinking. For application with traumatized clients, two methods of cognitive therapy are the most popular: cognitive-behavioral and dialectical behavior therapies.

Cognitive-Behavioral Therapy

Cognitive-behavioral therapy (CBT) is one of the earliest types of psychotherapy. It was popularized by behaviorists, most notably Joseph Wolpe, as an alternative to the analytical therapies of Freud and Jung. CBT basically targets the thinking process and helps the client to change negative thought patterns. Desensitization, a common technique for dealing with phobias, is part of the basics of CBT.

CBT holds that emotion is the result of thought. Therefore, if you change the thought you can change the emotion. Many of the therapies that have come after CBT adhere to this tenet in varying degrees. It is a deceptively simple concept that can be demonstrated simply by thinking about various situations and evaluating the emotional result. You can try it yourself: Just think about something you know was or is upsetting and see if your mood changes. Then switch to something pleasant and notice the effect. Because of the universality of this theory, many therapies include some form or another of attention to dysfunctional thought patterns, whether or not they technically fall into the cognitive therapies category.

Prolonged Exposure

The CBT method of prolonged exposure, sometimes also referred to as flooding, is the most researched and longest recognized specific therapy for trauma. In a sense, it was the first trauma therapy. The creator, Edna Foa, was the first to systematically use exposure to trauma memories as a treatment modality (Foa & Kozak, 1986; Foa, 1993). Basically, the model involves careful review of the traumatic event in every detail, often repeatedly. A common homework assignment is to continue to listen to a recording of the trauma memory on a regular basis. Desensitization to the memory is the expected outcome. While most subsequent models for trauma therapy rely on smaller doses of exposure, many find this method of prolonged exposure to the entire memory to be too difficult to manage. There are both documented and unofficial reports of high dropout rates for this therapy (Kubetin, 2003).

Dialectical Behavior Therapy

This is a great option for clients whose primary and most pressing need is to increase stability in their daily life. First developed to help those with borderline personality disorder, dialectical behavior therapy (DBT) is probably the only therapy in this list that exclusively addresses phase I issues. Therefore, it may also be a good choice for clients who do not want to work with memories but want to improve their quality of life. It is also the only therapy that utilizes structured group therapy in combination with individual therapy. Effective mindfulness (see Chapter 10), affect regulation, and increasing tolerance for distress are major goals of DBT.

Somatic Psychotherapies

The history of trauma therapy methods that include attention to what is happening in the body traces all the way back to the work of Pierre Janet in the late 1800s. It was Janet who first identified and described the phenomenon of dissociation and outlined the phase-oriented model discussed in Chapter 7. However, the legacy of working with the body in psychotherapy comes from Wilhelm Reich, the father of the vast majority of somatic psychotherapies practiced today. It was Reich who first worked directly with the body's responses to psychological states (1942). It is the work of both of these men that forms the foundation for the majority of the trauma-focused somatic psychotherapies.

Therapists and clients who are more in touch with or interested in the relationship of the body to emotions and thought processes will feel more at home with the somatic psychotherapies. Though there are exceptions, typically somatic therapies pay a good deal of attention to the mindfulness aspect of body awareness (see Chapter 10) and give greater opportunity for emotional expression and catharsis than cognitive therapies. Many, but not all, of the somatic-based therapies may still involve the use of direct touch by the therapist. However, since the turn of the 21st century, much greater discretion is involved in the use of touch. Many somatic psychotherapists (for example, myself) do not use touch as a part of treatment at all anymore.

To be successful with somatic therapies, clients need to have or be able to develop a keen sensory awareness of their own body. Those without a talent or capacity for body awareness may do better with a different type of therapy.

Somatic Experiencing

Peter Levine created somatic experiencing. His own influences include Ida Rolf, Wilhelm Reich, Stephen Porges, and Achter Ahsen, as well as ethologists and other scientists. His method aims to associate the disassociated elements of the traumatic experience, pulling together images, thoughts, feelings, behaviors, and body sensations into a coherent memory. By doing this, change in any of the elements becomes possible. People become able to think more clearly, move through emotions, complete behaviors, make sense of (and sometimes change) images, and so on, in resolving their traumatic memories. Levine's emphasis is on the key importance of completing movements (behaviors) that were prevented during a traumatic event. These are typically defensive movements involved in fighting or fleeing. In my experience of using aspects of this model, major change in any of the above-mentioned elements, including images and thoughts, may be equally powerful in promoting change (Rothschild, 2003).

Sensorimotor Psychotherapy

Developed by Pat Ogden, who was a student and colleague of both Peter Levine and Ron Kurtz (Hakomi therapy), sensory motor processing has many features similar to somatic experiencing (above) with greater emphasis on the integration of current neuroscience. Theoretical influences stem primarily from Bessel van der Kolk, Pierre Janet, Daniel Siegel, and Stephen Porges. In addition, sensory motor processing puts a greater emphasis on the therapeutic relationship, drawing heavily on the popular attachment research of the late 20th and early 21st centuries.

Bodynamic Analysis (BA)

Bodynamic analysis was developed in Denmark in the early 1980s by a team of Danish relaxation therapists headed by Lisbeth Marcher. Responding to the then-recent recognition of trauma as a separate category of emotional dysfunction, the Bodynamic trainers developed a specialized technique. Emphasizing the processing of the trauma memory, the Bodynamic running technique was created particularly to combat the freeze response by awakening the flight reflex through imagined running. It is a very powerful technique that works well for stable clients with noncomplicated traumas. However, it is contraindicated for some types of trauma and for clients who lack resilience. On the other hand, therapists trained in BA usually have a wealth of tools for helping fragile clients who are not able or willing to address trauma memories. So while the running technique may not be a smart choice for some, that does not rule out bodynamic analysis as a viable option for a good many traumatized clients.

Somatic Trauma Therapy

Somatic trauma therapy (STT) is the model that I have promoted over the years beginning with my first book, The Body Remembers (Rothschild, 2000). STT is highly influenced by my teachers, including Peter Levine, Lisbeth Marcher, and Bessel van der Kolk, as well as neuroscientists such as Antonio Damasio and Joseph LeDoux. Of course there are original elements, particularly my emphasis on common sense and the careful approach that I call "putting on the brakes." Janet's phase-oriented model (see Chapter 7) is a cornerstone. STT will appeal to those who are interested in (or good candidates for) addressing their trauma symptoms without delving into memories. For those who are ready and able, STT draws on many other models including somatic experiencing and bodynamic running technique (see above) and EMDR (see below). Transactional analysis (below) also figures strongly in this model (for a comprehensive overview, see Rothschild, 2000, and 2003).

Specialized Trauma Therapies

Many of the therapies below have been lumped into a category called "power therapies" throughout the trauma literature. As a whole, power therapies have been praised by some and maligned by others for claims of high levels of success in few sessions with little theory base to back up their methodology. I have flirted with many of them and trained in one. And I have listened to a great many of my colleagues, trainees, and clients rave about the usefulness of others that have not been attractive to me. So for these as well as every therapy offered now and in the future, both therapist and client must decide on an individual basis what to try and what ultimately works in each unique circumstance.

Neurolinguistic Programming

Neurolinguistic programming was developed from the observation of the best psychotherapists in the early 1970s. For the purposes of trauma work, their technique using the manipulation of submodalities is ideal for helping clients with intrusive sensory images (visual, auditory, kinesthetic). This therapy can help to change sensory input and increase control over symptoms. It is particularly suited for intervention with client flashbacks (Rothschild, 2003) as well as for therapists suffering from vicarious traumatization (Rothschild, 2006) (see Chapter 16).

Eye Movement Desensitization and Reprocessing (EMDR)

EMDR was created by Francine Shapiro specifically for work with trauma and PTSD. Roots include CBT and neurolinguistic programming. As it is also the only method outside of the strictly bodypsychotherapies to give significant attention to body sensations, it is a hybrid.

EMDR focuses on trauma memories and employs a protocol to gather together various aspects of the memory (image, thought, emotion, body sensation) and then facilitate change. It is believed that the active ingredient of EMDR is the bilateral stimulation that is applied while the client holds these various elements in consciousness. Following the therapist's finger with the eyes back and forth was the first type of this bilateral stimulation. However, in the years since its invention, EMDR stimulation has grown to include following a light, tapping on the knees, holding buzzers in each hand, listening to tones, and so on. The feature of all of these mechanisms is that they alternate stimulus from left to right repeatedly over about a minute's time. When that is finished, the client is asked what has changed in the basic aspects, and the procedure repeats from there until resolution.

EMDR will appeal to those who like the mechanics and primarily cognitive focus. It will not suit someone looking for a greater body focus or those who want to prioritize working on current issues rather than memories.

Energy Therapies: Thought Field Therapy and
Emotional Freedom Technique
These methods were both developed during the emergence of trauma as a legitimate field of study and treatment specifically to relieve the symptoms of PTSD. Both rely on a method of tapping acupuncture points in a specific sequence after identifying target issues or symptoms. Both of these therapies may appeal to some of those who cannot or do not want to go over their trauma memories. If the client has a knowledge of and belief in acupressure or acupuncture to begin with, these methods will make more sense and probably will have a better chance of being successful. Though originators and practitioners often claim that these methods have no negative side effects, they can and do certainly occur as with any other method.

Traumatic Incident Reduction
Another method that was specifically created for trauma, traumatic incident reduction was originally developed by Scientology trainers. Because of that association, it has had a difficult climb to be recognized as a legitimate method. It is highly dependent on processing trauma memory, often in a single prolonged session.

Additional Psychotherapies
Traditional methods of psychotherapy can be very useful for trauma therapy, contrary to the views held in the mainstream of trauma treatment. The emphasis on the therapeutic relationship (including trans-

ference) and on targeting attachment issues in these therapies have the potential to be very healing. They become even more valuable in the hands of a therapist who understands the basics of the physiology and psychology of trauma.

Psychodynamic Psychotherapy

A psychodynamic approach is at the core of many psychotherapies, particularly those which focus on the dynamics of the therapeutic relationship. Psychodynamics figure prominently in psychotherapy as it is taught today in many universities in the United States, particularly to those who become clinical social workers, counselors, and marriage and family therapists.

Usually, in psychodynamic psychotherapies, the client leads and the therapist follows the client's process. That can be great for the trauma client who needs to reclaim a sense of control. But it is not always the most ideal structure when working with trauma. Often clients are propelled into dysregulation or flashback while meandering through upsetting memories. Though it would seem alien for many psychodynamic psychotherapists to interrupt a client, that may be exactly what would be needed at such times.

Psychoanalysis

The father of all psychotherapies still has a place in the modern world of trauma treatment. Again, the important active ingredient in psychoanalysis for the trauma survivor is attention to the transference relationship with the therapist, particularly when there is childhood trauma perpetrated by caregivers. However, there is an important caveat. The core method of free association will be contraindicated for clients who are unable to contain their trauma memories or suffer from easily triggered flashbacks. Whereas many trauma therapies seek to help clients gain mastery over their memories, including when and how much they remember, free association could unleash the whole Pandora's box at once. As with any method, the psychoanalyst working with trauma needs to carefully adjust therapy procedures to fit the needs of the client.

Transactional Analysis

While transactional analysis was not developed for work with trauma, some facets of it are ideal as part of an integrated program of trauma therapy. The emphasis in TA on the internal dialogue has been adapted by several more modern therapies including voice dialogue, ego state, inner child, and so on. TA can be particularly helpful in facilitating the development of a caring and supportive inner dialogue between the part of the psyche that is highly functional and the part that was injured by trauma.

Equine-Assisted Psychotherapy

Horses have been used for decades to aid in the healing of various physical and emotional ailments. Into the 21st century, equine-assisted psychotherapy has grown more popular for helping PTSD. The Veterans Administration in the United States has even provided grants to investigate its usefulness for soldiers returning from combat areas. The therapy relies on the centuries-old bonding between humans and horses. Often the trauma survivor will create a stronger attachment to a horse than to a human, at least in the short term, gaining calm and relief from many symptoms along the way.

Hypnosis

While elements of hypnosis can be useful in trauma treatment, its use as a trauma therapy—particularly to attempt memory recall—has been called into question. When used to reduce symptoms, induce calm, and anticipate and rehearse future situations, hypnosis can actually be quite valuable. However, in decades past it was often used to help dissociated trauma survivors reclaim lost memories. In that usage, hypnosis has been implicated in the creation of false memories (see Chapter 13), much to the detriment of many trauma survivors. Research now is fairly conclusive that memories recovered under hypnosis are unreliable. Even more worrisome is the phenomenon that when someone believes he has recovered a memory with hypnosis, he will fiercely believe in that memory whether or not it is later proved to be false.

Expressive Therapies

Therapies that promote self-expression and creativity can be very helpful in healing trauma. Many such expressive therapies utilize the creativity of art, dance, music, writing, poetry, or drama, and so on. The idea of such therapies is to facilitate the client's emotional expression and cognitive organization through creative expression.

Nonpsychological Body Therapies

There are several methods of body therapy that advocate for or teach their students the treatment of trauma. Some specify their application as an adjunct to other, more psychologically oriented, therapies. However, there are several that claim that their graduates, even the ones who are exclusively trained in only their model, are fully qualified to treat trauma. Here I think a modicum of caution is advised. Though addressing the somatic aspects of trauma may be very important, addressing the psychological aspects is—at the least—equally important. So it is ill advised to approach trauma on a purely physical level. Psychological integration is a critically important element of healing.

Many of these methods can be extremely helpful for traumatized people—on an individual basis, as for any other treatment option. However, I would recommend that they only be used as an adjunct to a method that is psychologically oriented, either psychotherapy or body psychotherapy. Some therapists have training in both somatic and psychological theory and methods. However, those practitioners who only have somatic experience will often team up with a colleague who has predominantly psychological training. The team works together with the same client, each member applying their best tools, helping the client to integrate the two approaches. In such situations the resulting cooperative work can be very helpful.

In the list of helpful body therapies I would include cranial sacral, massage, Rolfing, shiatsu, Pilates, Feldenkrais, Alexander technique, and so on. Some of these are discussed in more detail in Chapter 11.

Brett and Jeffrey

The road to healing for many who suffer from PTSD will not usually consist of a single method or program. This was true for Brett and Jeffrey. Both their successful recoveries were owed to a combination of interventions. Their therapeutic programs differed significantly. In fact, their recovery paths are a good example of just how diverse therapeutic needs and tastes can be.

Brett first tried EMDR. It helped her to calm down and put the past rape into perspective. Though very useful, Brett felt she needed something that would help her more directly with her somatic responses. In particular, she needed to change her reactions when she found herself in sexual positions that reminded her of being raped. For that she found somatic experiencing to be of particular use. In tracking her process with it, she was able to follow some of the defensive impulses that were triggered in those positions. Eventually she was able to see the postures in the light of her current relationship instead of viewing them from her past. Last, Brett found a sex therapist who coached both her and her fiancé in regaining an up-to-date, normal romantic relationship.

For Jeffrey, the path was different. He was not interested in processing what had happened. In his early years of seeking help he had tried prolonged exposure but did not like it at all. His flashbacks were so disturbing, he found that anything that focused on past events made him feel worse. Eventually he found a VA psychiatrist who was intrigued by new research to try a short course of beta-blockers (see Chapter 9). That seemed to help, bringing down his chronic arousal levels. Encouraged by that success, Jeffrey was then referred to a social worker who taught him to use the neurolinguistic programming technique to control his flashbacks. Last, he participated in DBT group, where he learned more effective coping skills and gained greater tolerance for stress.

Psychopharmacology for PTSD

While many successful psychotherapeutic options for the treatment of PTSD have emerged in the last few decades (see Chapter 8), psychopharmacology options and outcome have lagged behind. The reasons for this discrepancy are certainly not due to study, as there is (and has been) plenty of research going on. However, the results of scientific investigation of PTSD to date are more along the lines of understanding the psychophysiology to a greater depth. There is markedly less success in terms of finding exact medications that will enhance, substitute for, or even be a better option than psychotherapy.

Part of the problem certainly stems from the difficulties faced by nearly every psychotropic drug. In the realm of the psyche, medication is just not as predictable and successful as it tends to be for treating many purely physical ailments. For example, antibiotics tend to work well and predictably for the specific bacteria they were developed to target; that is, unless the patient is allergic or has built up an immunity to that antibiotic. A wealth of additional medications for somatic diseases and complaints tend to have similar successes as well as cautions.

The picture is quite different with psychopharmacology. Medications within a particular category may or may not work well for an individual, and often several need to be tried before (if the patient is lucky) one works. Most patients with depression, for instance, will recount a history of multiple antidepressant attempts before finding one that works well. Often success is first realized when a combination of drugs is used, though the more numerous the drugs, the greater the chance for and incidence of side effects. And, as witnessed in the area of PTSD, medications designed for one ailment may be tried on a hit-or-miss basis with other ailments in the hopes of hitting a bull's-eye. Currently, for example, anticonvulsants, antidepressants, and antipsychotics are all being tried with PTSD even when depression, seizures, or psychosis are not concurrent diagnoses.

In general, medication for PTSD is not particularly effective. Estimates of success rates lie below 50%, which, though not terribly encouraging, is not unusual for this genre of medications. A specialist in psychopharmacology, Ronald Diamond (2009), advises that any particular medication for PTSD will show promise within the first few days of dosing. So if one does not appear to work within a week or so, it likely will not.

One of the first chemical substances to be tried for the treatment of PTSD was cortisol. Cortisol, as discussed in Chapter 4, plays a vital role in dampening the traumatic stress response when the threat has passed or been resolved. When it is able to be released in adequate quantity at the end of a trauma, it will halt the alarm reaction and reduce hyperarousal in recognition that the traumatic threat has passed. The release is directed by the limbic system, primarily the amygdala. In the case of PTSD, cortisol is not able to do its job to relieve the arousal. Those with the disorder have lower amounts of it in their systems following trauma than persons who experience the same trauma but do not develop PTSD (Yehuda et al., 1990, 1995). Why and when this failure occurs is still one of the mysteries of PTSD. It is a question that continues to be studied. This cortisol failure is a (if not the) major contributor to the development of PTSD. Therefore, because of cortisol's vital role in halting the trauma response and its low level in those with PTSD, it would seem logical to investigate its possible usefulness. Could it have a healing effect when administered to newly traumatized individuals after the fact or to those who have developed PTSD? Contrary to what one might expect, there are surprisingly few studies investigating cortisol's potential for aiding the healing of PTSD. Rachel Yehuda, the foremost researcher on the role of cortisol in PTSD, continues to promote further study of the use of synthetic cortisol as an adjunct in the treatment of PTSD while also, herself, questioning why more has not been done to date (Yehuda & Golier, 2009).

Encouragingly, there is another class of medication that could also hold particular promise. Beta-blockers act specifically on the chemical imbalances of PTSD. This class of drugs blocks the action of the adrenaline that is responsible for the typical hyperarousal symptoms of PTSD (rapid heart rate, blood pressure rise, and so on). However, the study of effects of beta-blockers on PTSD is still relatively new and there have not been many clinical trials as yet. The most interesting studies are being conducted by researchers in both the United States and Canada (Brunet et al., 2008; Pitman et al., 2002). See below for more on beta-blockers.

The following discussion highlights the most commonly prescribed substances in the treatment of PTSD. Beside each category, the most common brand names (if known) appear in parentheses.

Antidepressants (Prozac, Paxil, Zoloft)

The greatest amount of research on psychopharmacology for PTSD has been conducted with antidepressants, particularly selective serotonin reuptake inhibitors (SSRIs). Some SSRIs do have anti-anxiety properties and may be prescribed for anxiety. Though antidepressants help a portion of those with PTSD, there is also a large percentage they do not. Their success is sort of hit or miss, not unlike the track record of these same drugs with depression itself (Simon et al., 2006). In addition, some serotonin norepinephrine reuptake inhibitors (SNRIs), which increase levels of norepinphrine as well as serotonin, can also be effective in the treatment of anxiety. Mirtazapine (Remeron) is another type of antidepressant that has proven helpful with anxiety.

Prescribing antidepressants for PTSD has never made much sense to me. Of course when depression is underlying or concurrent, they may be useful. But it seems that regular use of antidepressants with PTSD remains in play as an intervention of last resort. Predictably, they are not terribly helpful when the primary problem is PTSD.

Benzodiazepines (Valium, Xanax, Ativan)

Drugs in this class are generally used to alleviate anxiety. Therefore, one might logically assume that they would be effective for PTSD, as it is classified as an anxiety disorder in the DSM. The opposite, however, appears to be the case. Benzodiazepines do not have a good track record with PTSD and, moreover, carry the risk of dependency, which can lead to abuse (Diamond, 2009). Benzodiazepines may be prescribed in the short-term along with antidepressants until the antianxiety properties of the antidepressant takes effect. The benzodiazepine would then be tapered off.

Buspirone

Unlike benzodiazepines, buspirone is an anti-anxiety medication that is slower-acting, without the risk of dependence. Like antidepressants, it can take several weeks to have an effect, and can be used to reduce anxiety.

Alpha-Blockers (Clonidine)

Generally, alpha-Blockers are prescribed to treat high blood pressure. Clonidine, however, has been prescribed for PTSD. It may be helpful in reducing hyperarousal and has also been shown to reduce intrusive thoughts and nightmares (Diamond, 2009).

Beta-Blockers (Propranolol, Inderal, Atenolol)

Hyperarousal is the first and foremost symptom of PTSD. The continued release of adrenaline as directed from the amygdala following a traumatic incident is the recognized cause of posttraumatic hyperarousal. It is, therefore, surprising that research on beta-blockers, substances that block the absorption of adrenaline (resulting in lower arousal) has been so scanty. As early as 1988, there was a small study of the beta-blocker propranolol in use with institutionalized children with PTSD (Famularo, Kinscherff, & Fenton, 1988). That study clearly demonstrated that propranolol significantly reduced PTSD symptoms in those children during the time it was taken. After that study, there is a striking absence of research into beta-blockers as a treatment option until around 2000.

Beta-blockers are a common group of medications usually prescribed for high blood pressure. On the psychological side, they are often used to manage stage fright and social anxiety. They have been around for a long time, and drug companies probably are less interested in experimenting with them because they are no longer as profitable as newer drugs. However, for PTSD, as discussed in the introduction of this chapter, they could have a great deal of potential. Studies to date have looked at the use of propranolol for the prevention of PTSD shortly following a traumatic incident (Pitman et al., 2002) and for the alleviation of PTSD, sometimes after many years of suffering (Brunet et al., 2008).

Morphine

Morphine is the drug being studied most recently for possible use to prevent PTSD. As with many important discoveries, this one was serendipitous. The potential for morphine to prevent PTSD was first noticed when observing psychological differences in wounded soldiers returning from Iraq and Afghanistan. A comprehensive study was conducted comparing the use of morphine to that of other medications. These investigations found that those who had been treated with morphine had about half the risk of developing PTSD as those who did not receive it (Holbrook, Galarneau, Dye, Quinn, & Dougherty, 2010). That does not mean that morphine will now be routinely prescribed for injuries. However, it could become more widely available to medics on the battlefield and could be used more readily in hospital emergency rooms.

Sleeping Pills

Part of the natural course of traumatic stress in the wake of a traumatic event necessarily involves disruption of sleep cycles. This is completely normal as it can take some time for a traumatized nervous system to return to its normal balance (homeostasis) (see Chapter 12 for a discussion on Nervous System Healing). When survivors receive ample care and support, sleep cycles will usually self-regulate after an individually determined period of time. Probably the most distressing facet of posttraumatic sleep disruption involves one or more episodes of nightmares as the psyche digests what has occurred. They are to be expected. If the trauma survivor can ride out these disruptions, sleep and dreaming usually return to normal on their own. When they do not, sometimes medication can be helpful. I would argue, however, that sleep medication is often overused in the aftermath of trauma.

Take, for example, the September 11, 2001, attacks on the World Trade Center in New York City. By the next day, many people were asking their doctors for sleeping pills and buying over-the-counter sleep aids. I question if that artificially facilitated sleep was useful. Since sleep medication can interfere with normal dream cycles, I would argue that they may delay integration of a traumatic experience. Unfortunately, there appears to be no study that tracked sleeping pill use, so this hypothesis remains unsupported speculation. However, during that time I observed the reactions of many people: my clients as well as my family, close friends, and colleagues. All of us had disrupted sleep for at least a few nights, some longer. None took sleep aids. As our nervous systems calmed and life, as well as sleep, gradually returned to normal, most of us had one or more periods of nightmares involving themes of the attacks. After a week or two, though, everyone's sleep had returned to normal and our dreams became ordinary once again.

Normalizing abnormal sleep in the wake of trauma can help an individual to ride out the distressing disruptions, making it possible for the body and mind to self-regulate and return itself to normal.

Recommendations

Please do not misunderstand my position here. When a person's body and mind are not able to self-regulate and return to homeostasis, appropriate medicinal intervention may be necessary and may prove very helpful. The correct medication in the correct dosage and the correct timing can be a godsend for some sufferers. If a client or therapist believes that adjunct medication may be helpful, then by all means, try it. But medication in lieu of trauma therapy is not recommended, as research also demonstrates that psychotherapy is more effective than medication for PTSD. When choosing someone to prescribe psychotropic medication, a good psychiatrist would be a better choice than a primary care physician. It will be particularly smart to select one with experience in treating PTSD and a good sense of what medications, and in which combinations, to try.

CHAPTER 10

Mindfulness and Meditation

Mindfulness meditation practice is both one of the oldest and one of the newest treatment options for trauma victims. It has played a major role in the psychological, therapeutic, and spiritual applications of many Buddhist practices as well as within other disciplines for thousands of years. Somatic psychotherapies have been applying the secular aspects of mindfulness for more than 100 years. Nevertheless, mindfulness has been reinvented in the 21st Century within the world of psychotherapy. In particular, relatively recently, the cognitive therapies have embraced mindfulness as one of their own. Daniel Siegel (2007, 2010) has been particularly instrumental in making mindfulness a legitimate addition to traditional psychotherapy practices. Moreover, many aspects of mindfulness are relevant for and helpful to trauma recovery whether undertaken in the course of self-help or trauma therapy. Because of the importance and growing popularity of mindfulness in the treatment of PTSD, this chapter is devoted to it.

Some confusion remains about the differences and similarities between mindfulness, meditation, and spiritual practice. Many therapists as well as clients shy from exploring mindfulness because they associate it with Buddhist philosophy. They do not recognize that in and of itself, mindfulness is totally nonsectarian. Actually, mindfulness is a part of many religious as well as nonreligious disciplines. There does not need to be any connection between mindfulness or meditation and any religion or spiritual pursuit for it to be useful to an individual. Major aspects of mindfulness can be employed to reduce stress and chronic pain (Kabat-Zinn, 1990; Miller, Fletcher, & Kabat-Zinn, 1995), manage depression (Segal, Williams, & Teasdale, 2001), recover from trauma (Rothschild, 2010a), and so on. Here the discussion is restricted to the relevance of applying principles from mindfulness to trauma therapy and trauma recovery.

Mindfulness

When you break down the term into its syllables—mind-ful-ness—what it means becomes clear:

- Mind refers to the psyche, the seat of our awareness.
- Ful means to be full of or characterized by.
- Ness denotes a state, quality, or condition.

Putting them together, it is evident that mindfulness has to do with a state of mind that results from filling the psyche with heightened awareness. In short, it is an active process that simply involves a purposeful focus of awareness or attention.

There are four main means to developing mindfulness, each worthy of its own focus alone or in combination with one or more of the others. There are numerous interpretations of these foundations. The following is a synthesis of the most commonly discussed features of each aspect:

1. Body awareness. This may include attention to the physical body, particularly via the breath and bodily sensations, as well as awareness of the energy fields in and around the body. It is this basic focus on the body that holds one's mindful awareness in the present moment.
2. Attentiveness to the quality of how an emotion feels in the body. This consists of both the sensations that accompany an emotion and its general impression: pleasant, unpleasant, or neutral. This aspect is also concerned with the recognition of the impermanence of emotions, how they rise and fall or appear, change, and disappear.

3. Attention to the mind. Included here are observations of mind states, feelings, thoughts, and images.
4. This final foundation has both secular and spiritual facets. Some regard it as having more to do with psychological health. In particular, it is concerned with the identification of obstacles to well-being. Others associate it with the spiritual side of mindfulness. In that regard, it encompasses the inter-relationship of all things in the world as well as guidance in living a moral life.

Of course, for trauma recovery, any feature can be applied, alone or in combination with one or more of the others. It is important to note that mindfulness can be highly useful as a part of a program of trauma treatment, even in the absence of any spiritual connection or connotation. Limiting mindful awareness to the first three aspects—body, emotion, and mind—can provide an extremely valuable tool in resolving traumatic stress and PTSD.

Because people who suffer with PTSD are so often pulled into the past, mindfulness and meditation can be a very powerful resource. They can give survivors concrete tools for strengthening their footing in the here and now, their present life.

Applying Mindfulness: A Personal Example

At this point, you might be wondering what it might look like to actually apply mindfulness in managing heightened distress. A few weeks ago, I faced some major dental work, the replacement of four 35-year-old crowns that were beginning to show signs of deterioration. The work was elective, but I agreed to it to prevent the worsening condition from becoming acute. Though I hate going to the dentist, fear the pain, and dislike the intrusion, basically I wanted to make sure to change the crowns before they fell out.

So, actually, that was my first step of using mindfulness: making the decision to have the work done. That step took several years. Periodically I would check back in with myself, observing my thoughts and feelings as I considered the current state of my teeth and felt my level of courage. Up until a few months ago, I was continuing to postpone the work; I was just too scared. However, at that time my position changed on two fronts: First, I became aware that the condition of the teeth was worsening. Second, when I held an image of dental work in my mind, I observed an increase in my feeling of courage.

I also used mindfulness to choose a new dentist. My previous dentist would have been adequate, but when I tuned in mindfully, I felt discomfort in my belly which was generated by doubts he was capable of this advanced work. So I visited several prospects and paid attention to my thoughts about their competency and also my belly sensations, feelings, and comfort level with each. When I left the office of the one I eventually chose, I was aware of actually looking forward to going back there—something I cannot recall ever feeling with regard to a dentist. That feeling, combined with my judgment of his competency, sealed the deal.

All of this careful, mindful preparation was important, but my next steps were critical to my successful emotional outcome. As the date arrived for the first appointment for the crown project, I began to notice that my anxiety level was increasing. Drastically. Though I no longer suffer from PTSD, I can still become quite anxious when faced with invasive and potentially painful dental or medical treatment. My anxiety rose so high that I became a bit worried how I would handle it all on the day of the procedure. Once again, mindfulness came to my rescue. A few days before the procedure, I purposely began to spend short periods of time (5 or 10 minutes) throughout the day involved in an intense mindfulness exercise. For me it was important to find my own way to exactly the mechanism that would work for me when I sat in the dental chair. Using a popular mindfulness tool, a body scan, I zeroed in on which part of my body I felt the most connection with. The purpose would be to keep me grounded by holding my attention on that part of my body instead of my anxious feelings or frightened thoughts. I chose my hands and my thighs. I would sit in a chair with my hands on my thighs focusing only on the sensations of my hands as they made contact with my thighs: their weight, their warmth, their solid feel. When my attention wandered or I began to feel anxious from thinking about the dentist, I would gently bring myself back to the sensations of my hands on my thighs. Sometimes I would move my fingers, rubbing them across my trousers so I could feel them on my legs through the cloth. At the same time, in my mind I repeated the words, "hands on thighs," over and over. Fine tuning this exercise to suit my needs in this situation was an optimistic last resort. I hoped that it would allow me to manage the appointments without freaking out.

When I woke up the morning of the first appointment, before getting out of bed I put my hands on my thighs and repeated, "hands on thighs," several times. Even while I was driving to the dentist's office, I repeated it (using only one hand, of course). This mindfulness exercise really did help to calm me down as I approached the medical building, even when my heart skipped a beat.

Arriving at the dentist's office, I made sure to tell him I was nervous. His response was professional, but kind and reassuring. That helped, but in no way banished my fears. I was still in need of mindfulness. During that day's 3-hour procedure, I repeated my mindfulness exercise many times, particularly during the first hour. When my anxiety rose up, I would remind myself to feel the warmth and weight of my hands on my thighs. After a while, I did not need to do it as much. All in all, I have to say the mindfulness exercise helped me immensely. I was able to get through the procedure without having an anxiety attack and without losing touch with myself or what was going on around me. Being able to manage my anxiety and keep my head also made it possible for me to respond to decisions, be assertive when something did not feel right, and say no when that was appropriate. I am very thankful for my knowledge of mindfulness for getting me through those (for me) very tough procedures.

Adaptation of similar principles, tailored to an individual's particular needs, will be helpful in managing heightened stress and PTSD symptoms without any kind of spiritual or religious connotations. For those who do want to weave in a spiritual component, that option is always available.

Meditation

Meditation is a discipline that employs mindfulness for achieving goals of varying types:

- Physical goals include relaxation, pain control, weight loss, and stress reduction.
- Psychological goals include quieting the mind, greater self-awareness, inner peace, reducing pathological behaviors (such as hyperactivity, depression, obsessions, and compulsions), development of compassion for oneself and others, gaining insight, developing creativity, enhancing intuition, and acceptance of life's unpredictability and periods of adversity.
- Spiritual goals include enlightenment, applying wisdom and compassion for self and others.

There are numerous different types of meditation, many related to spiritual practice. However, several basic types of meditation can be fused with mindfulness specifically to help PTSD. None of these basic types need be spiritually involved unless the person using them desires to add that dimension.

Meditation can be classified by physical position:

- Sitting. Varying postures are used in different meditation disciplines; you have probably seen a few of them. They can involve particular leg or hand positions. However, just sitting in a chair or on the floor in a way that is comfortable for you should be all you need.
- Lying down. The same principles as above for sitting. Find what is optimal for you. Remember that it is important to stay awake as one cannot be mindful when asleep. For that reason, lying down will not be a good choice for many people.
- Walking. Some people do not do well being physically still for a long period of time. They can get restless, dissociated, anxious, and so on. Walking meditation is a great alternative for those individuals. It can also be a very pleasant and useful meditative method in itself.

The types of meditation, below, are distinguished by their area of focus. Each can be done in any of the positions discussed above. In general, they all have the aim of quieting the mind, relaxing the body, and reducing stress.

- Breathing. This is probably the most basic of meditation methods. Attention is on the breath. It may involve breathing in a particular way or just noticing how it is and where in the body it moves at any moment in time.
- Body awareness or body scan. This type of meditation puts attention on body sensations, usually moving from one part of the body to another. The mindfulness exercise I used for the dentist evolved from this type of meditation.
- Topic. The person focuses on a particular thought or idea in the hopes of gaining clarity or insight. This may or may not be helpful for someone with obsessive thoughts. On the one hand, it could exacerbate the obsessive thinking. On the other, giving structured time to obsessive thoughts sometimes has the reciprocal effect of quieting them at other times.
- Guided meditations. Countless types of guided meditations

can be found in books, on CDs, and online. Some are spiritually oriented, many are not. A good many people like the structure of guided meditations; others dislike them. As with everything else, it is a matter of individual taste.

Caveats for Traumatized Individuals

Though mindfulness may be very useful to most people with PTSD, the helpfulness of meditation is not quite so assured. There are many with these conditions, as well as dissociation, panic, and anxiety, who may not do well with some types of meditation. This makes it important to find a good teacher who can instruct in many meditation forms. There is good news, though, for those individuals who cannot find a method that suits them at a particular point in their recovery. They may only need to wait until their symptoms are more under control and their base levels of hyperarousal have reduced. When they reach that point, they should try again. Often when general stress levels are reduced, previously difficult types of meditation become easier and more fruitful.

Eyes Open or Closed?

With the exception of walking meditation (for obvious reasons), meditation is usually practiced with the eyes closed. However, for many with PTSD and dissociative, anxiety, or panic disorders, closing the eyes may not work well. Some may be surprised to consider meditation with open eyes. Individuals should decide for themselves. Anyone who is unsure can experiment, alternating first one way and then the other. They can use mindful awareness of body sensations and emotions to decide which helps them to stay most calmly present.

Where to Sit

Meditation is generally practiced in a sitting position or sometimes lying down. Again, what is optimal should be determined individually. Include in that evaluation what kind of surface the individual is sitting or lying on. One person may do better with a firm foundation, while another prefers something soft. Many people with PTSD will find that sitting in a way that requires their back and neck muscles to support them (as in cross-legged on the floor, on a stool, or in a straight-backed chair) will prove more optimal than using a soft, stuffed chair or cushions.

Choosing Focus

It is not unusual for someone with a history of physical or sexual abuse to find that focusing on the body is distressing. When that is the case, choosing a mindful and meditative focus that is not body oriented may be the best choice, at least for a while. It is also possible to meter body focus, beginning with very short intervals. Some clients who would like to increase tolerance of body awareness still find that focusing on the body, even for a few minutes at a time, is too challenging. In such a situation, reducing the exposure to a span that is tolerable would be wise, even if it is only a second or two to begin with.

Calm Versus Relaxed

One of the usual goals of meditation is relaxation. Oddly enough, though, relaxation may be inadvisable, possibly even intolerable, for someone with PTSD, panic, anxiety, or dissociation. Individuals with these conditions likely account for the small portion of the general population (approximately 4%) who actually have a reciprocal reaction to relaxation. That is to say, they become more anxious when the body relaxes. This in no way implies that such individuals cannot meditate. It just means that they need to pay extra attention to how they meditate. For example, instead of lying on the floor with muscles completely relaxed, it might be better to stand or to sit in a chair holding the back straight. Optimally, there should be a period of experimentation to determine what is most advantageous for each individual. This relaxation phenomenon is discussed further in Chapter 11.

Mindfulness and the Trauma Therapist

Though this book is focused on the trauma survivor, it is worth mentioning the usefulness of mindfulness practice for the trauma therapist. I currently attend a monthly group with this focus at Insight LA in Santa Monica, California. The ongoing group, led by the center's founder, meditation teacher and former psychotherapist Trudy Goodman, has been helpful to many of us who work in the trenches with distressed and traumatized clients and supervise therapists working with the same population. One of the points that has been made again and again by the professional participants is how much their own embodiment of mindfulness affects not only themselves but also their clients. There are direct effects for therapists, including feeling more grounded and centered even when faced with extreme amounts of distress or conflict from their clients. And there also appear to be indirect effects as the calm of the therapist often gets transferred to the client. This may be a function of mirror neurons (discussed in Chapter 16). Nonetheless, it is a desirable result as a calm client can better integrate, and thereby utilize, psychotherapy.

Meditation and Mindfulness for Brett and Jeffrey

Brett had been practicing meditation for a couple of years at the time she was raped. Once her initial symptoms had resolved, she was able to continue her meditation practice as before. However, following the retriggering of her memories and the emergence of delayed-onset PTSD, she found that she was not able to meditate as she could previously. The few times she attempted it following her relapse, the mindful focus on her body would trigger a flashback. Losing her ability to meditate was nearly as distressing for her as the PTSD itself. She really missed it and the consolation and peacefulness it had usually brought her. Luckily her meditation teacher was informed about PTSD. Brett's therapist was open to finding a way for the three of them to work jointly. Together they helped Brett to experiment with different types of focus, posture, and seating. With their support, she gradually found adaptations that made it possible for her to return to meditation, though it was somewhat different than what she had done in the past. For instance, instead of sitting cross-legged on a floor cushion, she moved to a stool and kept her feet on the ground. She changed her attention from generalized body awareness to the feel and pattern of her breath. Last, she periodically utilized a guided meditation tape that she made together with her therapist. On it both she and the therapist recorded positive messages aimed at increasing her self-compassion and self-forgiveness and reinforcing her strengths and resources.

Jeffrey, on the other hand, had never been interested in meditation. He thought it was too "woo-woo" for him. However, the leader of the DBT group he attended recommended mindfulness meditation exercises for him to use. He acquiesced and was surprised to find that one of them was useful for him, though the others were not. The body scan became a valued adjunct to his recovery program, and he would aim to practice it at least a few times a week. Basically, he would scan over the surface of his body from feet to head and back again, paying attention to his sensations. He felt encouraged because while he was focusing on his body, his mind—and the accompanying guilt and other worries—was quiet. This mindfulness meditation exercise became like a half-hour oasis for him.

CHAPTER 11

Somatic Treatment Adjuncts

There are a multitude of possible adjunct activities and treatments that have the potential to assist traumatized individuals with their recovery. This chapter describes and discusses those that are most often used. Do not worry if your favorite one did not make my list. Absence of an activity or treatment in no way implies a negative view, only that there is not time or room to discuss them all. As with any other treatment options, the choice of what is helpful is highly individual. The more the trauma survivor can be encouraged to experiment with and evaluate various possibilities, the more likely appropriate alternative resources will be discovered.

In this chapter, the following treatment adjuncts are reviewed:

- Yoga
- Feldenkrais, Pilates, and Alexander
- Cranio sacral and Rolfing
- Relaxation training
- Strength Training

Yoga

Yoga is a time-honored mind/body discipline that originated in India many thousands of years ago. There are numerous types of yoga practice, ranging from the wholly meditative to purely exercise. Hatha yoga is probably the most recognized and popular in the Western world. It is identified by its many lying, sitting, standing—and sometimes rather acrobatic—postures and poses. Yoga practice is usually combined with some kind of awareness of breathing or breath control while various muscles are stretched and others are strengthened. Relaxation is the desired result for most enthusiasts.

Yoga is becoming a recognized adjunct treatment for PTSD. There is a young body of research to support its usefulness (Emerson, Sharma, Chaudhry, & Turner, 2009). Here a word of caution is warranted as a continuation of the discussion of the difference between relaxed states and calm states begun in the previous chapter. Yoga is one of the relaxation methods that has been discovered to evoke anxiety in about 4% of the population. So as with all interventions—psychological, somatic, or expressive—experimentation with careful evaluation will help to separate individually useful elements of yoga from the ones that are not so helpful or even hurtful.

Some years ago in my private practice I saw a rather dissociated young man who enjoyed yoga as a way to periodically "visit his body," as he would say. He liked the discipline but also had begun to notice that he was emotionally less stable since he had begun practicing yoga. It also became evident that several joint problems he complained of had their roots in the stretching yoga postures he had become accustomed to. He was desperately afraid he would have to give it up and despaired of how he would then handle his dissociation. We worked together to solve this dilemma. Ultimately, not only was it unnecessary for him to give up doing yoga, he was actually able to lengthen his practice time. The solution came from using mindfulness (see Chapter 10) to carefully observe the impact of each individual posture on his body, mind, and emotions. We made this the central task of several of his therapy sessions. Based on what we did together, he also learned to observe his responses to yoga on his own. In the end, with added input from his very helpful yoga teacher, my client was able to tailor his own individualized yoga practice program. Three areas were addressed: (1) He continued using some of the postures as he had been taught. (2) There were a few he had to stop doing altogether. (3) For the remainder of the poses, he made minor adjustments by reducing the amount of stretch, limiting how much time he spent, and so on. His mindful modifications continued until he had checked on every pose in his repertoire and the impact of his overall yoga program was neutral to positive (Rothschild, 2003).

Feldenkrais, Pilates, Alexander

All three of these body education programs—Feldenkrais, Pilates, and the Alexander technique—rely heavily on body awareness if they are to be practiced correctly. They are also taught to, rather than performed on, the student (in contrast to the treatments discussed in the next section). As such, they each can be valuable adjuncts to trauma treatment for those who find them helpful. Feldenkrais was developed to improve movement. Pilates specializes in increasing the strength of the body's core musculature. Alexander technique, originally developed to help those within the performing arts, specializes in improving posture and poise.

Craniosacral, Rolfing, Physical Therapy

These three—cranio sacral, Rolfing, and physical therapy—are all methods of body treatment. That is, they usually involve a trained practitioner performing a treatment on or to the body of the patient. While anyone assisting trauma survivors must be chosen carefully, when submitting to a passive treatment, the skill, knowledge, and respect of that practitioner are of the utmost importance. Luckily, there are many well-trained and competent practitioners. Nonetheless, caution is warranted. Unfortunately, there are also practitioners in these (and other) nonpsychotherapy body disciplines who believe themselves to be qualified to function as psychotherapists. This is somewhat understandable, as it is not unusual for psychological material to be triggered during these types of treatment. However, delving into psychological material, including trauma, warrants the professional skill of someone trained to treat those types of problems. Body treatments can be highly useful adjuncts, but they are not substitutes for necessary psychological care.

Relaxation Training

There are many types of relaxation training. For those with PTSD, there may be mixed results. Certainly there are many who benefit from it. However, it is also one of the causes of anxiety in that 4% of the general population previously mentioned. As discussed in the previous chapter, relaxation and calm are not necessarily the same thing. If the goal is to relax stressed muscles, then relaxation training may be a good choice. However, if the goal is to calm down, it may or may not be a good idea. Mindful awareness will help to identify the result for each individual. See the next section for an alternative to relaxation training.

Strength Training

In general, strength training is recognized as important for just about everyone, particularly as we get older. Increasing the strength and tone of muscles contributes many health and psychological benefits. Being stronger helps us to feel more in control of our bodies and environments. Strengthening exercise also releases endorphins and blows off stress. Besides needing increased power for their challenging professions, police, firefighters, and those in the military—whose work is very demanding and even potentially traumatizing—utilize strength training as a way to release stress and keep fit both physically and emotionally.

For someone with PTSD, increasing muscle strength could open the door to sanity. I have met many therapists as well as their clients who were distressed to find that relaxation exercises made PTSD symptoms worse. Oftentimes the therapist feels at a loss for what else to offer. I have also heard some professionals judge that failure to benefit from relaxation meant a client was being resistant. Likewise, it is not unusual for clients to despair they will ever get better when activities that "should" be helping, do not. In these instances, strength training could be a blessing. When relaxation fails, increasing muscle tone often brings relief. It can even work to help an insomniac sleep by enhancing the ability of the body to contain hyperarousal.

However, to be successful with PTSD, muscle toning must be done with a few caveats. First of all, the strengthening must be done at a low level of arousal, nonaerobic—that is, contracting the muscles, but without strain that would increase heartbeat and respiration. The reason for this is that sometimes elevated pulse and breathing can be a traumatic trigger, because the stress reaction at the time of a traumatic incident usually involves both. So keeping breathing and heart rate slow will decrease the chance of a trigger or flashback.

It is best to begin small and slow, picking one or two areas to strengthen. For example, push-ups may be chosen to increase strength in the arms, back, and chest. Begin with a position that is not challenging. For some, that may even mean starting with wall push-ups. Whatever is chosen, just do a few. Stop when the muscles begin to tire. It is counter to the goal of calming to repeat until the muscle burns. That is what you do if your goal is big muscles. In this case, however, the goal is to relieve anxiety. In that case, pushing the exercise to exhaustion could actually cause anxiety instead. Then, each day increase the repetitions at a gradual rate, always stopping when tiredness begins. It is also a good idea to keep track of the progress and the anxiety level pre- and postexercise as well as through an average day. That way it will be possible to evaluate if the strength training is useful.

It is also worth noting that increasing strength in one set of muscles might induce calm but in another set could induce anxiety. That is because no body is built the same. The distribution of more and less strong muscles throughout our bodies will be very different from one person to another. And which muscles facilitate calm or anxiety will also be different. Again, it is an individual thing.

Somatic Adjuncts for Brett and Jeffrey

Yoga was a natural adjunct for Brett. It dovetailed with her love of meditation. So long as she kept to carefully chosen poses, it was very helpful to her.

Jeffrey had no use for most of these options. But strength training appealed to him. Increasing his muscle tone helped him to feel stronger also in his mind and more in control of himself.

CHAPTER 12

How to Tell if a Treatment Works

Probably the most important consideration for both clinician and client when working together to heal trauma and PTSD is how to know if a course of treatment is actually benefiting the client. However, that brings up additional controversial questions regarding what benefit, healing, or cure mean to different people in various settings, cultures, and disciplines.

Essentially, the answer to the question of what works must come from the ones who are suffering, that is, the clients. It is they who will ultimately know if the help that is offered is actually helping. Of course there is a place for clinical observation. However, it is our clients who are the ultimate experts on themselves and who will be able to tell us what is and is not successful.

The Goal of Trauma Therapy

As mentioned in the preface, there is no goal for trauma therapy that is more worthwhile than to improve the quality of life of those who are suffering. This means improvement in life quality on a day-to-day basis, helping clients to function more effectively and be better adjusted in their daily lives. It may seem unnecessary to write something so obvious. However, in general, this is not the usual goal of trauma therapy as practiced. Take a look at the handbooks of most trauma methods and you will see that the customary therapeutic goal is to process the trauma memory. The prevailing philosophy is that trauma healing primarily (or only) results from reviewing the details of the traumatic incident. It is unfortunate—and too little discussed—that a significant portion of trauma victims do not improve from revisiting their past. Of course, a good many do, so it is absolutely reasonable to maintain memory processing as a treatment option. Still, a treatment intervention (which method or philosophy to apply) should not be the same as a treatment goal (feeling calmer, managing the stresses of work), though for some reason those two often are confused in the trauma treatment profession. Decisions about trauma treatment must be individualized since the means to and definition of a better quality of life will vary from individual to individual.

Who Decides?

It cannot be stressed enough that it must be the client who, in the end, is the one who determines whether a method, model, or course of treatment is helpful. However, this point of view may be at odds with an agency or practitioner who only has one type of therapeutic intervention, one method, to offer. Sometimes professional adherence to a single method is due to personal style preference. At other times it is because of belief in the evidence base. It could also be because of restrictions of a workplace or third-party payers. No matter the reason, it is highly recommended that clients choose practitioners who are trained in multiple therapy models and treatment organizations that provide several to choose from. That way, if one intervention is not productive, there will be plenty of flexibility to try something else.

The emphasis on evidence-based practice (see Chapters 7 and 8) has (inadvertently) drastically limited treatment options in many settings, particularly HMOs. This is regrettable as, despite the evidence, no "proven" method appeals to, or works for, every client. It does not even make sense to expect it to be otherwise. Unfortunately, the policies of a particular agency or setting may require clinicians to use modalities that do not suit them or that they just plain disagree with. It would be much better for both client and clinician if decisions about the treatment direction, including which methods would be applied, could be made within that relationship, with multiple options available to sample and choose from. Because of my publications, I get regular calls and e-mails from clients looking for a trauma therapist and asking advice for how to choose a practitioner and a method. I generally tell them, "Just because all the evidence in the world says that method X is the best in no way guarantees it will work or be good for you. So make sure that your new therapist has training in at least three methods. That way, if one doesn't work well for or appeal to you, it will be possible to try others." The commonsense bottom line: No one method, model, or strategy is for everyone.

There are several concrete indicators with which to evaluate both success and failure of trauma therapy. Of course, those discussed below will not cover all possibilities. In fact, within any good therapy the therapist and client should decide goals and identify likely indicators of progress and regress together. It will also be helpful to predict how they will recognize them. To begin with, the therapist might keep a record of the symptoms that brought the client to therapy and evaluate along the way if those symptoms are improving, getting worse, or staying the same. Discussing symptoms and goals at the outset will help to ensure that individualized criteria are available for future evaluation.

Symptom Profile

Which symptoms does the client have at the outset of therapy? Always consider at least the following:

1. Daily functioning:
   - Does the client follow a normal routine?
     — Rise in the morning
     — Go to work or school or tackle the day's usual chores
     — Have contact with friends and family
     — Keep to a reasonable bedtime
   - To what degree is eating normal or disturbed?
   - Are sleeping patterns disrupted?

2. Trauma specific:
   - What is the frequency of intrusive thoughts or images about the trauma?
   - What is the intensity of intrusive thoughts or images about the trauma?
   - How frequent are trauma-related nightmares?
   - Is concentration disturbed?

3. Affect management:
   - How is affect regulated?
     — Self-soothing

— Reaching out to others
— Alcohol or drugs
— Dissociation
— Other
- How long is the period from upset to eventual calm (see How the Nervous System Heals, below)?

Questions clients can use to take an inventory themselves before and throughout a course of therapy include asking if, on a day-to-day basis:

- Am I more or less calm?
- Has my ability to concentrate improved or weakened—on a task, conversation, book, television program?
- Have my mood extremes lessened or increased?
- Have the rate and frequency of flashbacks or other intrusive experiences decreased or increased?
- Am I more or less able to deal with normal daily challenges?

Triggers

Trigger is the common jargon used to describe anything that provokes a trauma survivor into a traumatized state. The reaction can range from a slight increase in anxiety to a full-blown flashback. A trigger could be anything that reminds the client of the trauma and will be individual to that client and that trauma. Psychologically, triggers are conditioned stimuli from the trauma.

Do you remember Dr. Pavlov's dog? The doctor wanted to train his dog to salivate at the sound of a bell. So he first showed the dog some meat, waited for it to salivate, and then rang a bell. After doing this repeatedly, all Pavlov had to do was to ring the bell and the dog would, indeed, salivate.

Trauma triggers work somewhat the same way. A sound, smell, color, object, body position—just about anything—present or active during the trauma can become conditioned to it. So, for example, someone who was caught in a terrorist bombing while drinking orange soda in a café might later on become frightened at the sight of the color orange, or the taste of the beverage, or the feel of fizz on the tongue. In that case, the orange soda would have become a conditioned stimulus to and reminder of the bombing, a trigger to the memory.

One of the most important goals of trauma therapy, and one way to evaluate its success, is the reduction of the impact of triggers on the client. Sometimes a trigger will lose all effect. But for most triggers, their effect will be dampened increasingly over time. On the other hand, when triggers maintain their power to activate a strong and lengthy trauma response, therapy has not yet been successful.

SUDS, A Useful Gauge

In 1969, Joseph Wolpe, the famed behavioral therapist, introduced his Subjective Anxiety Scale. He would ask patients to rate their anxiety levels on a scale of 0 (no anxiety) to 100 (the maximum anxiety possible). The reported number became known as the SUD, the subjective unit of disturbance. In recent decades, trauma therapists have been adapting the SUD scale (SUDS) to assess the immediate state of distress of their clients. Many now also use it for evaluating the progress and outcome of both individual therapy sessions and the course of treatment.

Now, usually based on a 10-point scale, the SUDS is very simple to use. All that is required is for the client to estimate the level of distress by choosing a number from 0 or 1 to 10. The lowest number would indicate absolutely no distress; the highest being the worst possible distress the client could imagine. The SUDS can also be used to plot progress. For example, 0 is no progress at all and 10 is the most progress possible. In this way the scale can be adapted to apply to just about any kind of evaluation or tracking the therapist and client might want to do.

Remember, though, that the scale is, as its name implies, subjective. As such, it is a valuable indicator but should not be used as the only marker. Objective (observable) criteria should also be included for a full picture both during a session and for evaluating a therapy overall.

Objective Evaluation Criteria

Observing behavior is the main way to objectively evaluate the progress or regress of a client. The observation can be made by the therapist, by family and friends, and especially by the client. Things to look for include the following.

How is the client functioning in comparison to when therapy started? Is she better able to fulfill her roles in her life, family, and culture? For the family wage earner, that would mean, for example, going to work and earning a living. If the client is a stay-at-home mom, the criteria would include managing the home, shopping, food preparation, and child care. Children and teenagers have different things to measure: Getting up in the morning, doing well in school, completing chores at home, and enjoying normal activities with friends would all be important factors to pay attention to.

Subjective Evaluation Criteria

While observing behavior and tracking symptoms are important in evaluating successful therapy, do not forget to include the client's own perception.

- How are you feeling?
- How do you think you are doing?
- Are you satisfied with your progress?
- Is there anything you feel is missing from your treatment?

These are all useful questions to ask from time to time. Remember, it is ultimately the client who must be the final judge of the success or failure of trauma therapy. It is important for the therapist to ask. And it is equally important for the client to periodically give the therapist an evaluation, whether asked for or not.

How the Nervous System Heals

There is another important factor to figure into any evaluation. A severe shock to the nervous system does not heal completely from one day to the next. It tends to be a gradual process. Even when a person recovers on his own, it may take time. Think about your own reaction, for example, in the wake of the attacks in New York on September 11, 2001. Were you completely calm by the next day? My own initial reactions took many days to normalize. Any mending from trauma requires a healthy dose of patience. In many cases, traumatic stress will continue to be triggered. With PTSD, this may go on for a long time. Still, as the nervous system calms there will be noticeable differences. Below are some clues to what to look for and how to measure changes.

It will be useful for both the trauma survivor and the helping professional to take note at the beginning of therapy: Just how long does it actually take for the client to get equilibrium back once provoked by a trigger? For someone with PTSD, initially this could take a long time, even days or weeks. For others it could be merely hours. Each situation is different; the important thing is to establish a baseline. How is it for the client initially?

Then, no matter which phase of therapy is the focus, phase I, II, or III (see Chapter 7), continue to gauge changes in the time it takes to wind down after getting triggered. Take note if there are differences depending on the trigger, or if there is an overall pattern. The main thing to pay attention to is that the time span does change. An increase could be an indicator that something is amiss in the therapy, something is going wrong. On the other hand, as the client's state improves, the distance between triggering hyperarousal and return to a basically calm state will get shorter and shorter.

This is important for both clinicians and clients to realize as either or both can become frustrated when triggers continue to provoke upset. When after months of conscientious work a trigger still has force, it can seem like a stalemate or even regression. It is when it is recognized that the time between trigger and recovery has, indeed, reduced—sometimes greatly—that an incident of triggering can be seen as progress instead. The most important mark of healing is that these intervals wane.

Adding this information to your overall understanding of trauma can put a sensible spin on healing: emotions and arousal get easier to regulate over time. It is not reasonable to expect never to be upset again. Life just does not work that way. Everyone has upsets and distress at times. What determines emotional health—and trauma recovery—is how those stresses are handled and how quickly one bounces back.

At some point during trauma therapy, nearly every one of my clients has complained following an incident of life distress that they felt they were moving backward. There is a tendency to describe and be upset about such a reaction as, "Just the same as it used to be. Nothing's changed!" When I suggest that they compare how long it used to take to recuperate from such an upset with how long it takes now, they are often amazed to realize that they really have improved—often greatly. "Oh, that used to take me days. This time I was only upset for 2 hours." The goal is not to be 100% free of trauma reminders. They may continue to be an integral part of the client's history. Instead, the aim is to maintain or quickly recover stability in the face of those reminders.

Revisiting Brett and Jeffrey

The main goal Brett set was to be able to again enjoy sex with her fiancé without having flashbacks or unsettling physical symptoms. Anything sexual had become a trigger. Her progress was very slow and gradual. Luckily, her fiancé was so in love with her that he had a huge capacity for patience. With the guidance of a therapist, Brett and he again got to know each other physically step by step. While in therapy Brett worked on the psychological issues; at home she took control of the contact. For example, for a period of time their only physical contact was holding hands. Once Brett could do that without triggering memories or symptoms, she added in kissing, and so on. Each step was toward her ultimate goal and the evaluation was fairly easy as the goal was clear.

On the other hand, Jeffrey was not so clear about what he was aiming for. All he could say was, "I want my life back!" It was difficult for him to nail down exactly what that meant. Partially that had to do with his stage of life at the time of his trauma. He went straight from high school into the army. He had not really established an adult life outside the military. He did not know what he wanted. However, he did have obvious symptoms, as described in Chapter 2. During the years he was in and out of VA hospitals, his symptoms persisted, some even getting worse. Unfortunately, it appeared that the available treatments within the VA system were not working for him. Because of limited resources, no one offered him alternatives outside of the military, though there was no way of knowing beforehand if any of those would be useful to him or not. As mentioned in Chapter 8, he did, at last, find a psychiatrist who was a good fit for him. The success of the beta-blocker seemed to help him turn a corner. When the nervous system arousal reduced, he could think more clearly and was in a better position to make use of further interventions introduced by his social worker.

CHAPTER 13

Common Issues Inherent in PTSD

O course every individual is unique, including those who experience trauma. Therefore the issues, and the treatment, of any one person must be planned and tailored to the needs of that individual. At the same time, a number of issues are common to those who suffer in the wake of trauma. A discussion of these will be useful so long as you keep in mind that even though the issues in this chapter usually accompany PTSD, they will still manifest and need attention in individual ways.

Control

Trauma only happens when an individual is not able to control the situation, is not able to prevent the threat. This is true whether the trauma is a natural disaster, accident, or intrusion or injury at the hands of another. If the incident could be averted or reversed, there would be no trauma. Therefore, anyone suffering from trauma or PTSD knows intimately what it is like to be out of control. Further, the persistent characteristics of traumatic stress increase that experience of being out of control in the form of the distressing physical and psychological symptoms that are the hallmarks of PTSD. Probably the most disturbing aspect of PTSD is those symptoms themselves. In this way, the feeling of being out of control follows trauma survivors into their daily lives, affecting their self-concept and degrading their quality of life. It is therefore that regaining a sense of control must be a central aim of any trauma therapy or program of trauma recovery. Control must be reestablished in multiple ways, both small and large. This may include, for example, the choice to leave on a light at night, install additional locks on doors and windows, learn dual awareness or mindfulness to modulate arousal levels, and so on. It may require extra patience from the trauma therapist as well as friends and family to easily swing with the needs of the trauma survivor for increased control. When, for example, a spouse has been sexually assaulted, there may be a need to control the sexual arena for at least a period of time (as Brett did). This can be difficult for the partner. Parents who are trying to help their traumatized children may need to be more flexible and give more choices to help their children to feel more in control (for issues such as picky eating, the need for a light at night, or not wearing certain colors). These special needs often require a great deal of patience. It is possible that family members or even friends could need therapeutic support to manage both the knowledge of their loved ones' traumas and their increased need for control.

Working to better control stress symptoms will go a long way to heal trauma whether or not the memories themselves are ever addressed. And, in fact, symptom control is a necessary prerequisite (phase I) before addressing memories (phase II). Gaining mastery over trauma symptoms will ensure that memory processing has a better chance to be successful and manageable. It is always advisable to begin phase II work from a place of stability and self-control. In general, attention to control issues usually pays off with a greater degree of security, inner peacefulness, and improved quality of life.

Support

Contact and support have been demonstrated as major components in both the prevention and healing of PTSD. The therapeutic relationship—or any relationship with a helping professional, for that matter—certainly can be counted as a portion of posttrauma contact and support. However, a therapist should not be the only support for the trauma survivor. This is an area where I have often seen one of the more key mistakes widespread in trauma therapy: neglect of the client's network. It is critically important that a good portion of therapeutic time be spent in helping clients to better relate to friends and family, also in the context of the traumas they have experienced. Sometimes the therapy is so overly focused on the past that the importance of the present gets missed or lost. This can be very costly for the client. Often in the aftermath of trauma, survivors feel very alone and isolated. They may feel as if no one could possibly understand what they have experienced. This is one place where trauma therapy can actually be a huge help: coaching survivors in how and when to talk with others as well as how to ask for, recognize, and utilize support. In some cases, securing ample support and contact will be all that is necessary to prevent or heal PTSD. In other cases, it will create a fertile, nurturing environment where recovery becomes more easily possible.

Shame and Guilt

Feelings of shame and guilt are nearly universal in people suffering from trauma. One or the other, or both, may be in the foreground or background along with the other pertinent issues. In a previous book, 8 Keys to Safe Trauma Recovery (Rothschild, 2010a), I related the story of Chesley "Sully" Sullenberger, the pilot who safely glided a US Airways flight to safely ditch in the Hudson River in January 2009. A bird strike had killed both of the plane's engines. Even though he accomplished a nearly impossible landing, saved every life with merely three serious injuries to passengers and crew, Sullenberger felt guilt in the aftermath. He told 60 Minutes' Katie Couric, "One of the hardest things for me to do in this whole experience was to forgive myself for not having done something else, something better, something more complete." It occurred to me while listening to him, and still seems relevant now, that if he—who acted as a true savior—could feel guilt about what happened, then shame and guilt must be inherent in the wake of most any traumatic event to nearly every person.

So both therapist and client should be on the lookout for shame and guilt. Those feelings deserve attention as a part of both phase I and II work. However, timing (as with all things) should also be a factor. Often such emotions are among the most difficult to deal with. In many instances it will be wise to tackle them later rather than earlier in the course of recovery. Still they are necessary components of the ultimate integration of the experience of trauma.

In psychology it is commonly accepted that guilt is related to an action, having done something wrong. "I should or should not have done. . . ." Shame, though related, is somewhat different, deeper in a way. It usually has to do with a more integral feeling of being wrong in some way. "There is something wrong with me."

Most psychotherapies have no particular structure for identifying and paying attention to shame and guilt. However, eye movement desensitization and reprocessing (EMDR) (see Chapter 4) does include indirect attention to these emotions as part of its protocol that targets the processing of trauma memories. A key element in the EMDR procedure is to ask, "When you think about that trauma (or element of it), how do you feel about yourself now?" This question zeros in on what EMDR calls the negative cognition. Usually, that negative thinking is tied to shame or guilt: "I am stupid." "What's wrong with me?" I believe this is one of the key elements of EMDR that provides a major contribution to its success. How we feel about ourselves now in relationship to something that happened then reveals just the kinds of disabling thoughts and emotions that may be keeping an issue or memory unresolved—usually shame or guilt.

Nevertheless, it is not necessary to use EMDR to elicit connections to those feelings and issues. Often feelings of shame and guilt will be obvious. But even when they are not, the therapist can certainly ask about them. However, it is best to set the time for working with these difficult emotions on an individual basis. It should never be pushed onto the client. It will also help to keep in mind this useful caveat: Never tell a client, "You have nothing to feel ashamed about." People feeling shame have a negative reaction to such a well-meant message. It could even increase the feeling of shame or guilt, adding the weight of thinking, "What's wrong with me for feeling this way when my therapist says there is no reason for it?"

Above, in the section on support, I mentioned how people with PTSD tend to feel isolated and alone. It may be that shame and guilt figure strongly in this tendency as they are also highly isolating emotions. You might recall a time when you felt very guilty or ashamed. Did you want to be with others or by yourself? Withdrawal is a universal impulse when feeling that way. This feature of shame and guilt also provides a guideline in how to help heal them: contact. Both shame and guilt are more easily managed in the context of acceptance and understanding than in isolation. When alone, they tend to grow further and further out of proportion. Support helps bring guilt and shame into perspective and helps them dissipate where possible.

False Memory Risk
I deeply wish that a discussion of false memory were unnecessary in this book. It would be wonderful if at this time in the evolution of traumatic stress studies it were no longer an issue. Certainly we have

come a long way as a profession in recognizing and preventing many potential risks for the creation of false memories. However, it continues to be a problem at this writing, so the following discussion is still essential.

A few readers may yet be unfamiliar with the history of the false memory controversy, and so a bit of historical perspective is warranted. The False Memory Syndrome Foundation was founded in the early 1990s to defend a number of people (usually parents) who were accused of sexual molestation or incest by adults who believed that they had recovered childhood memories of such abuse. There ensued a huge uproar in the trauma field that is still not completely resolved. There are fanatics on both sides of the argument, some asserting that any emergence of abuse memories must be true (the so-called recovered memory movement) and others who believe that only continuous memories are valid and that abuse cannot be forgotten (the false memory adherents). Probably most professionals in the field of traumatic stress stand, as I do, somewhere in the middle of the road: On the one hand I have witnessed that abuse memories can, indeed, be totally repressed and later emerge with more or less accuracy. On the other hand, it is also evident that false memories of abuse are a legitimate danger when care is not taken to hinder their formation.

Because of the danger of false memory, we as a profession have learned (often the hard way) that it is never a good idea to work with suspected memories of abuse. A good example comes from my own practice. Albert, a 30-something man, came to me on self-referral after reading one of my earlier books. A couple of years prior, he had begun to suspect he had been molested, possibly even raped, by a family member when he was a small child. He was waking at night in a panic, and he became more and more reticent in sexual contact with his lover. The therapist he had seen prior to me assumed the suspicion was accurate and began processing it as if it were confirmed fact. Within a few weeks, Albert found himself becoming more and more distressed and less able to manage the sexual side of his relationship. At the point where he broke off contact with his lover, he began to suspect that something was going terribly wrong and left that therapy.

Albert was extremely anxious when he appeared for our first meeting. Not only had his relationship dissolved, but he was increasingly having difficulty at work. Per usual, I took a complete history, including both medical and trauma history. He knew he had been in the hospital when he was around 5 years old with a serious bacterial infection. He did not know any details but was willing to ask his mother for more information. It turned out that during that hospital stay he had had periods of delirium and had been given ice and alcohol baths in an effort to reduce his dangerously high fever. His mother related several incidents of his having been hysterical while being bathed.

It was my suspicion that the hospital incident could be a significant trauma and could be adequate to account for his feeling as if he had been abused—even though it was clear that the treatment in the hospital was for the purpose of saving his life and was not intended to cause him further suffering. Albert and I discussed the prospect that his 5-year-old fevered mind may not have been able to distinguish life-saving support from abusive intrusion. It was possible that this incident was at the core of the feelings that had plagued him, that he had diverted to the idea of molestation or rape by a family member because he did not know how to account for them otherwise. This is quite common, especially when early medical treatment is involved, though there can certainly be other explanations. Identifying his hospital experience as a possible source of his feeling of abuse, Albert calmed considerably. It made sense to him and cleared the way for Albert and his very loving and patient lover to get back together. Eventually, all suspicion of sexual abuse disappeared and Albert was able to get on with his life and relationship.

Ongoing Trauma

I cannot emphasize this too strongly: Do not work on trauma when the client is still in a traumatic situation. This is one of the most vital rules of thumb for processing trauma memories and the emotions that accompany them. Many people endure ongoing traumatic circumstances as a part of their daily lives. It could be, for example, that they:

- Live in a family plagued by domestic violence (a battered spouse, an abused child)
- Live in a war-torn country or a violent neighborhood
- Struggle with a life-threatening illness
- Are involved in a legal process to adjudicate a perpetrator

Any of these or similar situations would qualify as ongoing trauma. That is, the end point of the event or events has not yet been reached. It is not time to sigh with relief. They cannot say, "It's over, I survived," because it is not over yet. Of course, people in such circumstances are suffering, so why shouldn't the therapist work with the cause of their suffering, the trauma?

All psychotherapists know that defense mechanisms are coping strategies. We develop them to help us to manage through adverse times and situations. They help us to handle what might otherwise be intolerable. Defense mechanisms are numerous, effective, and vital to our emotional and psychological survival. People surviving daily with ongoing trauma are people who are particularly adept at developing coping skills. They need them. Without their defenses to help them through, a person living in ongoing trauma could be in greater danger.

And that is where the problem lies. Survivors of ongoing trauma desperately need their defenses. At the same time, opening up to processing trauma and the affects that accompany them will loosen defenses. It is not possible to work with traumatic material without a loosening of defenses; that is the only way to resolve it. That is why trauma therapy is a bit tricky in the first place and further explains the wisdom of stabilizing in phase I before moving on to phase II (Chapter 7). At the least, opening up to the impact of trauma would cause greater instability. At the worst, it could risk breakdown or put the person in greater physical danger. Though most psychotherapists are not also physicians, the vast majority would agree with the Hippocratic Oath that our first duty is to "never do harm." For that reason, trauma therapists cannot risk depleting a client's coping skills by inappropriately opening up the Pandora's box of their trauma memories and emotions.

So, if you cannot work on past trauma with survivors in trauma, what can you do? Lots of things, including these:

- Help them to strengthen their defenses and coping strategies.
- Enhance their healthy contacts and support.
- Strategize emergency planning.
- Help them express and contain their emotions about what is happening now.

Anything that helps to increase their safety and ability to cope will be useful.

Brett and Jeffrey

Both Brett and Jeffrey had issues of control. As discussed previously, Brett needed to be in charge of her sexual contact for a period of time.

A step-by-step approach worked well for her. For Jeffrey it was more a matter of controlling his symptoms in ways other than use of drugs and alcohol. The DBT group he attended was particularly useful to him in this regard.

Of course, they both also had feelings of shame and guilt to struggle with. Brett agonized over restricting sexual contact with her fiancé. She felt guilty that she might be making him suffer because of her own trauma. She also felt ashamed for how she had been treated in the hospital following being raped. One thing that helped her very much was the realization that it actually should be the hospital personnel who should have been ashamed for not taking her disheveled distress seriously. Jeffrey had a serious internal battle with survivor guilt. The fact that he had survived when his buddies had not was difficult to bear. However, in his VA support group, he discovered that many of the other veterans had similar feelings as they all had witnessed the deaths of buddies during combat. Normalizing his guilt feelings helped enormously.

What About Prevention?

Of course, most traumatic events cannot be prevented. By definition, trauma is usually something that is unexpected and catches you off guard. However, there are a few situations in which one can anticipate, prepare for, and thereby avert trauma and possible PTSD:

- Scheduled medical interventions, including surgery
- Anticipated loss such as when a loved one has a terminal illness or will undergo a hazardous procedure
- Military personnel facing active duty
- Bank employees
- Others in high-risk jobs or with high-risk hobbies and their families

Anticipation and Planning

When a situation that has potential to be traumatic can be anticipated, the best way to minimize or prevent PTSD is to plan for it. In particular, dealing with serious medical issues, surgery, and other invasive procedures is very amenable to such measures. On my very first social work job in the mid-1970s, I had a client who was facing surgery. She was panic stricken. It was not the procedure itself that frightened her, but she was totally freaked out with the thought of the anesthesia. As a child, she had been traumatized by the application of anesthetic for a tonsillectomy. She awoke confused, shocked, and feeling very, very alone. She was terrified of revisiting those feelings upon awakening from the upcoming operation.

Because the date was imminent, we did not have the luxury of being able to work through the feelings and memories of the childhood surgery. The task was to figure out what to do as she confronted this similar scenario. I was new on the job and not at all versed in dealing with trauma. At the time it was virtually unrecognized (remember PTSD first appeared in the DSM in 1980). But my common sense kicked in and I was inspired to help my client to prepare for a different outcome. With my encouragement, she talked with her doctor and also the anesthesia department at her hospital. Her direct honesty was well received and they were able to acknowledge and give her support for her fears. She also obtained permission for her husband to be in the recovery room when she woke up, which was not usual in those days. Together we were able to zero in on exactly what she needed, and she was able to tell her husband what to say, precisely what she needed to hear, as she was waking up. The most important for her was to be oriented on who he was ("I am Joe, your husband"), where she was ("You are in the hospital"), what was happening ("You are waking up from anesthesia following your surgery"), what she was experiencing (Probably you are disoriented and queasy"), how she was doing ("Don't worry, you are just fine"), and, finally, his feelings ("I love you, sweetheart, and will stay here to help and support you"). Even their communication about this was a step to healing for this client. As a child, she had no warning of the impending tonsillectomy and, therefore, had no chance to talk with anyone about it. There had been no way to prepare for or soothe her fears.

When the time came, all the groundwork paid off and her surgery and recovery all went off without a hitch. She had still been afraid and upset, but it was a completely different experience. She knew what was happening and was aware of the support of the doctors and her husband. Though unpleasant, it was bearable. Of course it was frightening, not to mention painful, at times. But because of her preparation and the support she had rallied, it was not traumatizing, and there were no lingering effects of PTSD for this incident. She still had a bit of work to do on the childhood scenario. However, when we revisited that some time later, so much had been resolved by the better, more recent experience that the earlier incident was fairly easy to deal with and lay to rest.

Rehearsal

Do you remember fire drills when you were a kid? Every school has them. They are not intended to be the free break from studies and routines that children often regard them as. Actually they are meant to prevent trauma. The more you practiced lining up, being quiet, marching to the street or far side of the playground, the more automatic it would be in the unlikely event of an actual fire. Fire drills are meant to reduce panic and thereby possible injuries by making safety procedures habitual, able to be followed without thinking. They train the limbic system's amygdala to be able to tell the body what to do at the prompt of the teacher's instruction or a sounding bell. In that way, making sure you get to safety can bypass the need for the slower cortex route to process the information before setting a response in motion. This kind of rehearsal saves loads of time and promotes safety.

The same idea can be applied in anticipation of other types of stress and trauma. Firemen, soldiers, police, and so on all repeatedly practice the procedures designed for their (and others') safety. The idea is to make sure they too can respond automatically in stressful situations. In addition, rehearsal and practice can also reduce stress during an emergency so that clear thinking might also be possible.

Another good example of this comes from the aforementioned January 2009 incident known as "The Miracle on the Hudson," when pilot Chesley "Sully" Sullenberger safely dunked his jet that had suffered the loss of two engines due to a bird strike. He had practiced such procedures during training simulations as both a commercial and glider pilot many times. Rehearsing emergency landings is a usual part of pilot training, though most flyers never need to call on those talents. So Sullenberger had the necessary skill sets embedded in him. When the time came, he knew in both mind and body what to do. His reactions were composed and automatic. He was so well rehearsed that he was able to stay cool to make the decisions necessary about where to go. "We'll be in the Hudson," he calmly, but firmly, told air traffic control. And so they were a few minutes later, everyone still alive, with less than a handful of injuries. Rehearsal saved them all and won Sullenberger the gratitude of his passengers, crew, and their friends and family. Moreover, though there are scattered reports of passengers and one crew member who did eventually develop PTSD, the rate appears to be far lower than what one would expect from such an incident. It is likely that both Sullenberger's training and the safety rehearsal of the crew served to also reduce eventual PTSD.

You and your client can do the same. For instance, have fire drills with your family. If you live in an earthquake-, tornado-, or hurricane-prone area, practice how you will respond when one hits. Don't just think about it, actually do it. Let your body experience where you will go and the posture you will assume. Practice your procedure enough times that it becomes automatic. If your client works in a high-risk job, advise him or her to ask to be allowed to actually practice procedures rather than just hearing about them in a lecture. It will also be important to refresh such practice at regular intervals.

Prebriefing

Having knowledge of trauma and how it might affect someone—in advance—can be sanity saving in the event of a traumatic incident. This will be particularly relevant for those in jobs where trauma is a strong possibility, such as being a soldier or bank teller, working in the police or fire department or on oil rigs, and so on. Learning about the psychology and physiology of trauma will make it possible for an individual to know what to expect, what is normal, and what might require professional help. For example, a victim of trauma should expect to be hyperaroused, to have trouble sleeping, to be upset or dissociated, and so on in the aftermath. It will also be important to remember that those same difficulties will gradually reduce on their own over a (usually) short period of time. Knowing that such symptoms are normal could help keep individuals and communities from panicking. It could also reduce incidence of sleeping pill or other drug and alcohol abuse following trauma.

For those who live or work in high-risk situations, it could be very useful to create a plan book to use in case of trauma. In such a book people lay out plans for what to do and whom to call, and add reminders of what to expect physically and psychologically. Keeping a list of supportive friends and family alongside phone numbers can be extremely helpful at a time when memory could be compromised. It can also be reassuring for newly traumatized persons to see they have written lists of possible disturbances they may be experiencing, for example, of appetite or sleeping. It will be an added bonus if comforting suggestions are also written in the book, such as these:

- If you are reading this, you survived.
- Remember to breathe.
- You won't be feeling this way forever.

Self-Defense Training

Though it will not provide perfect protection, self-defense training can go a long way in preventing PTSD. It can also build or restore self-confidence and an increased sense of security to those who are healing from trauma. Learning self-defense will be particularly relevant when someone is recovering from any type of physical or sexual assault.

Probably most kinds of boxing or martial arts will be useful. However, there is a particular type of self-defense training that has an impressive track record for enabling men, women, and children to effectively protect themselves against many types of assault. This program was founded under the name Model Mugging in the mid-1980s. You may have seen films or pictures of women attacking fully padded and helmeted attackers who look much like the Michelin Man or Darth Vader. The method originated following the rape of a female karate black belt. At the time, others in the martial arts community were concerned that one who was so adept could also be so vulnerable. They first questioned, then investigated, what specific skills were needed to thwart bodily attacks of all sorts. Eventually they developed a system that is designed to teach people step by step specifically how to defend themselves. Currently this method is taught under two names: Model Mugging and Impact. Both organizations have centers in many places in the United States and elsewhere in the world. Their trainers can also be hired to travel to other locations.

Stress Management

In the last couple of decades, mindfulness has experienced a resurgence in popularity as previously discussed in Chapter 10. It can be a huge help in mediating stress whether from the past, in the present, or anticipated for the future. In particular, Mindfulness Based Stress Reduction, the program developed by John Kabat-Zinn and popularized in his book, Full Catastrophe Living (1990) will go a long way to equip most people to better manage stress of all kinds, including traumatic stress. However, people with PTSD should review the meditation caveats on page 96, and those on yoga on page 100, as both play a major role in MBSR.

Friendly Fear

This may seem ludicrous to some of you reading this, but making peace with feeling fear can be one of the best protections an individual can have against trauma and PTSD. In general, all of our emotions are there for a reason. As uncomfortable as it is to feel, fear, in particular, plays a major role in survival. It is fear that will alert you to the possibility of danger. When your heart begins to race and your palms break out in a cold sweat, your body is telling you that this is a good time to look around where you are and pay attention to what you see, hear, and smell. There is a good possibility that your amygdala has just registered something from your external environment that could signal danger. When there is an immediate threat to life, you may not be aware of feeling fear until after the fact, as it is your amygdala's job to push your body to flight, fight, or freeze before your cortex is aware of what is happening. But when you have the luxury of time, you will likely feel scared first.

Of course, it will be particularly difficult for people with PTSD to see fear as a friend. In many instances, they are feeling afraid most, if not all, of the time. Moreover, because of chronic fear, those with PTSD (as well as anxiety and panic disorders) often tend to assume that there is some sort of menace in the environment, perhaps perceiving danger everywhere all of the time. These people have lost the ability to use fear as a protective mechanism. When one is always afraid on the inside, it becomes impossible to use external senses to actually identify true danger or, for that matter, safety. Refer to the Chapter 4 discussion on exteroceptors and interoceptors and their role in dual awareness. When survivors are able to distinguish their sensory input, allowing internal sensations to define internal reality and their external five senses to define external reality, fear has a much better chance to fulfill its protective function. Then avoiding at least some dangers becomes possible.

First Aid

As with any kind of injury, physical or psychological, appropriate first aid helps people to survive in the short term. When properly measured and applied, it can sometimes prevent the need for some—or even all—further treatment.

Much of trauma therapy involves traumas that happened in the past, often a long time ago. However, sometimes an individual will seek therapy immediately following a traumatic event or a current client will encounter a traumatic incident while being involved in a course of therapy. There is also a significant number of clinicians who sign on with the Red Cross and other helping agencies to be first responders to catastrophic events such as house fires and plane crashes, or massive events such as the attacks of September 11, 2001, the 2004 Indian Ocean tsunami, Hurricane Katrina, or the devastating Haitian earthquake in 2010. In these instances it is important to understand that the type of help that is appropriate for past trauma may not be at all appropriate for a recent occurrence.

Invoking Maslow

In the immediate wake of a traumatic incident, individuals first need copious amounts of support and attention to their basic needs. This may include—as was the case, for example, after Hurricane Katrina and the Haitian earthquake—medical care, shelter, food, financial assistance, help with locating loved ones, and so on. Even when the trauma is on a lesser scale, the immediate aftermath is not the time for what one would normally construe as therapy. Following recent trauma, clinicians may find they need to adapt their role, sometimes to help clients find appropriate agencies to access and provide critically needed services. Such steps may be absolutely necessary before a client will be able to utilize psychological help. I shudder when I hear of trauma therapy being quickly offered on a mass scale to disaster victims. It seems that Maslow's (1954) hierarchy of needs can get forgotten in the enthusiasm to heal trauma. But it is important to remember that it is the items at the base of Maslow's triangle that must be in place before attempting psychological work. The triangle's foundation is composed of physical needs such as food, water, and air. The next level involves safety, including shelter and protective clothing. After that comes social needs, including contact from family and friends. It is actually the top of the scale, the last stage, the one that involves personal growth, where trauma therapy is appropriate. We humans only have a true capacity for psychological development once our basic needs, those at the lower levels of Maslow's Triangle, are met.

So when therapists volunteer as responders to a natural disaster or take on clients who have fled a war-torn country, they must adjust their usual professional priorities. In such cases, the first things to be attended to are the foundational needs. All trauma therapists need to take care that they are not in too much of a hurry to do trauma therapy. If so, they just might be overlooking pressing, practical needs such as jobs, networks, or even adequate food and shelter.

Essential Emotional Support

When basic needs are not an issue, therapy may still not be the best approach or even appropriate. It may be that a client just needs someone to be present and listen rather than to intervene. As a young therapist, I learned this the hard way. I look back with chagrin on my behavior with two particular clients, one who had just lost her husband and another newly diagnosed with cancer. In my newbie clinical enthusiasm, I leaped to my brilliant treatment strategies when all that each desperately required was just a hand to hold, to cry, to ramble. Neither lasted long in therapy as, despite my good intentions, I was not paying attention to what they really had need of: my support and reassurance, not my techniques.

On the emotional side, what is needed in the first response to trauma is contact and support. This cannot be emphasized too much. Over and over again in both research and practice, contact and support are shown to be the major mediators of traumatic stress. It is those who receive the most appropriate and adequate emotional support who will be the least likely to develop PTSD. A somewhat extreme example will illustrate this tenet.

With all new clients I gather a comprehensive history, no matter the reason they are engaging my services. Some years ago a young woman came to my office seeking advice and guidance. In the course of our initial interview and history taking, she revealed that in her teens she had been gang raped. For anyone such an incident would be extremely traumatic, no less for her. However, as she talked about it she seemed fine, as though she was resolved and peaceful. She was not without feeling, but obviously stable and clear. Her composure and poise in speaking about such a horrendous event surprised me when I factored in that she had never had professional help from a therapist or a rape crisis center. Up until that time I had my own therapeutic prejudice that anyone suffering rape, let alone gang rape, would need therapy to come to terms with it. How was it possible she had come so far without clinical intervention?

Curious, I asked her what factors had led to such a successful recovery. At that point her eyes began to water and she cried softly. These were not the tears of terror, desperation, or even anger. What provoked her gentle crying was a touching memory. Her best friend, who was still her best friend, had been the first person she contacted after getting free of the rapists. The friend rocketed to her side and stuck to her like glue through the entire and lengthy aftermath, including police, hospital, lawyer, court, return to high school, and normal activities— through it all. Moreover, her friend was often whispering in her ear just the kinds of messages that any of us would need to hear through such an ordeal: "I love you just the same"; "It was not your fault"; "You will get through this and be just fine"; and so on. More than anything else, it was the friend's contact and support that helped this young woman through that nightmarish time. And, looking back on it as an adult, it was the friend's support that was the stronger emotional memory for the young woman.

Of course, not all of our clients have this kind of support system. And many who end up in our offices do so because of the absence of adequate support. Sometimes the clinician is, at least temporarily, the sole support system for the trauma survivor. However, whenever possible, it is important to help your clients to access and engage their support network, be that friends, family, pets, clergy, or whoever might be available. Sometimes it will be necessary to help a lonely soul to construct a support system. Time spent in that pursuit is extremely valuable. When that is the most pressing task, I sometimes find myself in the role of coach, helping my client to figure out and be successful at identifying, making, and keeping one or more friends.

Out of Isolation

It is difficult in the wake of trauma for survivors to reach out for support. Many will tell you, "No one can understand what happened to me." In that way, trauma can be extremely isolating. One of the best and most helpful things you can do for your traumatized clients—actually those with both recent and past trauma—is to help them talk with friends and family. Teach them how to talk with others about their feelings and experiences. A critical element will be helping them learn how to judge who will best be able to listen to various aspects and themes. Any way you can help your client to be better able to identify and utilize supportive others will be highly beneficial. It will also be helpful to coach the client in timing, learning when is a good time to discuss emotionally intense topics and when it might be better to focus on lighter themes, even small talk. Sometimes trauma survivors will be so preoccupied with their issues that they burn out a previously useful network because they do not know how to take breaks from the heavy issues. Help in this area could be an essential part of your therapeutic work. Contact and support are integral to recovery throughout the healing process (throughout life, really) whether dealing with something current or historical.

Contact and Support Lower Arousal

As mentioned, we have plenty of evidence that adequate support and contact in the immediate wake of traumatic events can prevent, or greatly reduce, PTSD. Recently it has occurred to me that the mechanism that makes it successful might be similar to how the beta-blockers, discussed in Chapter 9, work by reducing the action of adrenaline. Both beta-blockers and contact and support reduce stress and hyperarousal; people calm down. When survivors get adequate amounts of these following trauma, perhaps they just do not generate as much adrenaline as someone who is isolated by trauma. This would be an interesting area for research.

Controversial Debriefing

Critical incident stress debriefing (CISD), developed by Jeffrey Mitchell (1985, 1986), was very popular in the 1970s through much of the 1990s. However, toward the end of the 1900s its usefulness began to come into question as studies emerged showing mixed results from debriefing. Some of the research demonstrated that participants in debriefing had a smaller risk for developing PTSD; other projects indicated exactly the opposite. The question of whether or not debriefing should be used at all became a huge controversy in the professional field of traumatic stress (Devilly, 2003; Robinson, 2008). I have yet to find studies that analyzed the differences between these debriefing programs, but I would wager a good deal that those that emphasized support of friends and family had the better results.

As discussed in Chapter 7, not everyone benefits from reviewing what happened during their traumatic event. This may account for some of the failures of CISD, as central to the model is recounting the details of the trauma in a group setting. Moreover, the direction of communication during the debriefings is from the individuals to the leader, the debriefer. So the amount of direct contact and inter-support is actually very minimal and the emphasis is on what happened. I believe that it is these two central features of traditional debriefing that could account for the low incidence of success reported by independent researchers.

What If Brett And Jeffrey Had Better First Aid?

Let me remind you about the aftermath of Brett's trauma. You may recall that she was brutally raped. She was able to flee the rapist while he slept and made her way to a hospital emergency room. Unfortunately, that ER was having a very busy night and the staff was overwhelmed. They did not prioritize Brett's situation and she had to sit for more than 30 minutes before anyone attended her or let her use the telephone. That was a very long half hour for her. I have wondered how the clinical picture would have been for Brett if someone at the hospital had recognized her distress as urgent, taken her seriously, listened to her, and helped her call her parents and best friend. If Brett had received the support she needed immediately, would that have been enough to prevent the later development of PTSD? Of course there is no way to know, but it certainly cannot have helped Brett's physical and psychological state to have to wait under very disheartening circumstances.

Jeffrey's situation was quite different. In actuality he did receive a good amount of support quickly and then consistently over a long pe-riod of time. However, it was not always just the kind of support he needed. Of course his superiors were interested in getting him back on duty as soon as possible. For that reason, much of the early interven-tion was pointed in that direction. This was not the approach Jeffrey needed. So though support was available, it missed the mark. More-over, it is possible that, unconsciously, Jeffrey did not want to return to active duty. He was in no hurry to risk seeing more of his buddies die.

Vulnerability and Self-Care

Whichen I conceived of this book, I included this section on self-care with only the therapist in mind. Therapy with traumatized clients often exacts a greater toll on the emotional, and sometimes physical, reserves of the therapist than working with other types of clients. Midway through my writing, however, I realized that in this chapter I also needed to speak to the clients, including supportive family and friends of traumatized individuals. In truth, they are equally at risk—perhaps even more so—for the same vulnerabilities as the therapists. Anyone who cares about and supports a traumatized individual or individuals is at risk of being infected by the traumas they are hoping to help to relieve.

The reasons for this are complex, but they are rooted in the palpable impact that trauma has on the victim's nervous system in combination with the vulnerability of the empathetic therapist or other supportive person. There may be some people who feel little or no negative impact from lending support to the traumatized, or perhaps they are only affected rarely or in minor ways. However, over the many years I have been supervising and training therapists in working with trauma and advising those in a client's support system, complaints of anxiety, excessive fatigue, unmanageable countertransference, and burnout abound. As well, often the therapist will hear clients talk about (or complain of) friends or family members having adverse reactions when trying to listen or give other kinds of support. The difficulties seem fairly universal. The most extreme situations involve those who begin to feel they are traumatized as much as the victim, sometimes having similar symptoms and even nightmares of the survivor's trauma, despite never experiencing anything similar. Many practitioners find it more difficult to leave such clients at the office, often finding themselves more irritable, upset, or tired than usual on days they see particular individuals or deal with specific issues. For friends and family, it may become difficult to think about or feel anything besides the trauma of their loved one. The daily life quality of one or more in a client's supportive network may begin to decline.

A variety of terms are used to describe the difficulties someone can have when helping and supporting traumatized people. Compassion fatigue was coined by Charles Figley (1995) to describe the emotional and physical exhaustion that one can suffer from giving compassionate assistance. Vicarious traumatization is used when another experiences symptoms of traumatic stress as if he were the victim of the trauma himself (McCann & Pearlman, 1990). Burnout is a general term applied in many areas of the working world to caregivers, employees, or workers who have overextended their reserves to such a point that they can no longer function properly in their role (Freudenberger, 1974). Those suffering burnout may also find their private life affected. Some are just so exhausted that they lose their joie de vivre: Life is not fun anymore. Burnout can be a problem in nearly anyone in every walk of life including stockbrokers, lawyers, teachers, and so on as well as helping professionals, parents, and friends. However, it is primarily clinicians, caregivers, and family and friends of traumatized people who are in danger of compassion fatigue and vicarious traumatization.

Vulnerability

Many factors can increase one's risk for compassion fatigue, vicarious trauma, or even burnout. Whether you are a professional or part of the survivor's supportive network, it is a good idea to take an honest inventory of both your personal and professional lives. Focus on trauma can make it easy to ignore basic needs. While you are helping another in a personal or professional capacity, do not forget to get adequate rest, eat sensibly, take care of any of your own psychological or health issues, and make sure to take time off. That is probably stating the obvious. However, bear in mind, many people who are good at helping and supporting others are often not so adept at doing the same for themselves. If you forget about yourself while you are taking care of another, you will put yourself at huge risk for both psychological and physical consequences. The cost could be great, including interference with your ability to help that person or others in the future. Here is a good rule of thumb: The better you take care of yourself, the more and better you will be able to help someone else and be able to maintain that support.

So, for example, make sure to take time to pursue other activities. Therapists should also have clients who are not dealing with trauma. Keep a balance in your practice so that you are not overloaded by tragedy. Friends and family, make sure to keep contact with your own support network. Take time to continue the activities and contacts that are important to you. And take time out. That may mean a week or more off for the practitioner or a break of some days or evenings for the friends.

In Red Cross lifeguard courses, one of the first things they teach you is that if you are getting pulled down by the person you are trying to rescue, fight for release and then swim away. On the surface this may seem like a cruel instruction, as it could mean that person drowns. But think about it. If you drown with that person, you'll never be able to try to rescue anyone else. So it is not cruel—it is necessary as well as potentially beneficial to those in the future whom you will live another day to help.

Self-Care for Professionals

Much of your best support will be found in supervision and colleague consultation. Those who are tackling many of the same difficulties as you are will also be a great source of consolation and insight. Unfortunately, too many workplaces have drastically reduced the amount of postlicense supervision. And because many employers require their therapists to see too many clients per day, time for collegial interaction may be limited or even nonexistent. When I was a new social worker in the 1970s, nearly all agencies required a minimum of 2 hours per month supervision for those who were licensed. New therapists had supervision weekly. Agencies also had more reasonable expectations for client hours and allowed time for us to write up our notes and consult with each other during our working hours. It is a shame that these same types of agencies have become so pressured in the last couple of decades. As mentioned above concerning lifeguard training, the first line of care should be for the caregivers. I hope those professionals reading this will, where needed, put pressure on your workplaces to take a more humane attitude toward the needs of the staff. And you are welcome to quote me from this book as well as Help for the Helper (Rothschild, 2006).

Empathy: Friend and Foe

Empathy involves the capacity to feel our way into another's experience. When I empathize with you, I feel what you feel. It facilitates our understanding of others and helps link us together in relationships. Generally, empathy is neither good nor bad—it just is. It is an automatic process; it either happens or it does not. I think of it as a double-edged sword having obvious benefits as well as underrecognized risks. Do not worry. I am not going to advise against empathy. I know it is our number one resource as helping professionals. However, by the end of this chapter, I will have made a case for tempering that sword by making empathy a conscious process, and learning to increase the advantages and decrease the disadvantages of empathy at will.

The Neuroscience of Empathy: Mirror Neurons

Mirror neurons were first identified in the mid-1990s by brain researchers in Italy (Gallese, Fadiga, Fogassi, & Rizzolatti, 1996). As with many critical discoveries, this one was accidental. These scientists were actually studying grasping behaviors in monkeys. They recorded the firing of neurons when the monkeys would grasp for a piece of food. Amazingly, one day during a break a researcher reached for a piece of food and the grasping neuron in the monkey fired then too, even though the monkey was sitting still and only observed the action of the researcher. It was as if the monkey's brain felt the grasp in the same way as when the monkey made the movement itself.

This discovery set off a wildfire of excitement throughout the neuroscience world. What did it mean for a neuron in one brain to fire in response to action from another as if it had made the action on its own? In brief, it could mean very much for our understanding of communication and community. The observing monkey more than saw or even recognized the researcher's movement. It actually felt it as if it had reached and grasped itself. That is one aspect of empathy and one of the directions that mirror neuron research has taken. Others include the role of mirror neurons in the development of communication and language and the possible absence of a mirror neuron system in those with autism. It is an exciting, growing area of neuroscience.

For our purposes here, the implication of mirror neurons in understanding empathy is the most relevant. Mirror neurons appear to facilitate empathy. When we observe another crying and our own eyes tear up, mirror neurons are a part of that process. Reflexive smiling and yawning involve mirror neurons. And the feeling of fear and restricted breathing that can grip someone listening to the trauma of another may also be the mirror system at work.

The Benefits of Empathy

For anyone who helps others, empathy is our major, greatest, and most reliable tool. Whether you are a helping professional or an interested friend or family member, empathy allows you to understand the experience of others, to have a sense of what they are feeling. For the psychotherapist, empathy also helps you to put your clients' past into perspective by having a deep understanding of how their history is affecting them in their daily life and in the therapy room. Empathy helps us to relate on all levels. It enhances our insight, increases the accuracy of our hunches, and sometimes even helps us to seemingly read another's mind. Psychotherapists and counselors would be lost without empathy. And in its absence, we would not form relationships— friends and family. Our capacity for empathy is critically necessary to our social lives. In research studies, helping professionals generally show a greater aptitude for empathy than the general population. It is one of the things that preprograms us to want to help. However, empathy is not always our best friend.

The Risks of Empathy

At the same time that empathy helps us to resonate with "good" vibes, it also makes us potentially vulnerable to "bad" vibes. That is, the same mechanism that helps us to share joy with our friends also facilitates our sharing in their pain. Have you ever felt uncharacteristically or unexpectedly nervous in the presence of someone who was anxious? Or has another's anger also infected you to the point where you became angry about something you had been more neutral about, or angrier than you had been in the first place? How about this: Are there movie scenes that make you cry, your heart pound, your muscles tense, or turn you on? All of these reactions are mechanisms of empathy. Anytime you are sharing in the experience of another, whether pleasant or unpleasant, in person or at the movies, empathy is operational.

The benefits are fairly obvious. Empathy facilitates humans to care about and support other humans. It helps us to form family and friend groups, bond, help each other, and work together toward common goals.

Disadvantages of empathy may be less apparent. However, it is this same mechanism that is, for example, at the root of riots and mob violence, the power of charismatic dictators, the glue of cults, and so on. Empathy is also at work when we find our good mood has disappeared from being infected by the distressed state of another.

When dealing with trauma, empathy can wreak havoc on the helping professional, the support network, and, for that matter, the traumatized individual, especially those who participate in a debriefing, support group, or group therapy situation. The terror, horror, anxiety, panic, images, and sensations of a trauma victim can all be taken on by someone else if they are not paying attention. So, for example, if you are helping someone who has been raped and you begin to feel as afraid of walking to your car as she is, you might be infected. When you are helping a victim of a natural disaster who is confused and hungry and you find yourself confused and unusually hungry, your empathy dial may be turned up too high. And if you are having the same nightmares as your friend, client, or loved one, then you have caught their trauma as surely as you can catch influenza from someone who is ill.

Decreasing Empathy's Sting

This book, Trauma Essentials, is meant, as its subtitle says, as a go-to guide. That is, it is an overview of the most important theory and treatment options for helping people with PTSD. As such, it is not meant to teach techniques. However, in this final chapter I cannot resist offering readers a few mechanisms for reducing their own empathy risks. Hopefully, including the following sections will help all readers to be better able to care for and support traumatized individuals. For the survivors reading this book, these strategies may help you to better prepare your network to support you and assist you in helping others you may encounter who have also been trauma victims.

It may be helpful for you to think of empathy as being controlled by a dial. Turn the dial up and your empathy goes up; you feel more of what the other person is feeling. Turn the dial down and you gain distance from whatever is going on with the other person. You gain the ability to think more clearly and be objective about what you can and cannot do to help when your empathy dial is turned lower. Both directions of the dial have advantages and disadvantages. As well, one direction or the other will be most appropriate in varying circumstances. If you experiment and practice with turning your empathy dial up and down, you will probably find that a spot somewhere in the middle is ideal in most circumstances. That will be the place where you can feel with the other person enough to know what is going on without your own clear thinking being overwhelmed by resonance.

What do you already know about maintaining an objective distance from another's upset? Whatever tools and resources you already have for that will be helpful to remember and apply now. Nevertheless, you could probably do with some additional inspiration.

Imagery

Even those of us who specialize in trauma theory and treatment are not immune. I was painfully reminded of this fact recently. When I first heard that a good friend of mine had been a victim of violence, held for a period of time with a gun to her head, I knew I felt sad for her, and also relieved that she had survived. Other than that I was not consciously aware of any shock to my system. The reaction came later that night in the form of undifferentiated insomnia. Since I had heard the news about my friend earlier in the day, I did not connect my sleeplessness to trauma, but tried to find other reasons for my wakeful state. Eventually I got to sleep for a few hours, but awoke cold and shivering. I was actually shaking so strongly that I checked to see if I had a fever. To be honest, it is a bit embarrassing to admit that it still took me a while to connect my shivers, sleeplessness, and underlying distress to the news I had heard the day before. Once I made the connection, everything calmed and I felt more myself again. Later, talking with another friend, I remarked that it was humbling to realize just how vulnerable I, too, could be even with all that I knew. But there it was, vicarious traumatization from hearing the news of my friend's encounter. It did not last long, only those 18 hours or so. But it reminded me just how strongly any of us can be affected by the trauma of those we care for and care about.

What made me so vulnerable? There could be many factors, but two stand out. The first is that this was someone I related to on several levels. Though we do not have a lot of contact, she is in my sphere and I am fond of her. The second is that as I heard the news I immediately—and seemingly involuntarily—had a sharp visual image of her in that situation. Unwittingly, I was strongly reminded that imagery is a very powerful mechanism for taking another's trauma into one's own (in this case, my) system.

One of the most protective things you can do when listening to someone recount trauma—their own or another's—is not to visualize what the person is saying. That is, do not make pictures in your mind's eye or try to imagine the sounds in your mind's ear, or try to feel in your body what it must have been like. Of course, as I did, you might do this automatically. But it is worthwhile to become aware of any tendency you have to create imagery. This type of empathy is extremely risky when you want to make sure you are not infected by the other's trauma. The more fully you imagine their experience, the more likely you will feel traumatized as well.

For those who resonate with images, sounds, or body sensations automatically, it will take some practice for you to reduce and eventually stop this habit. I know that many of you reading this will protest that it is the only way for you to relate to the other's experience. However, consider this fact: Unless you were there and experienced the same thing, the images, sounds, and sensations you create in your own mind and body are only—at best—a guess of what it was like. Those images are not really what happened.

Controlling visual imagery has several options. First of all you need to know if you:

- Visualize in first person (as if it is happening to you)
- Visualize in the third person (as a witness)
- Are prone to visualizing what happened to you or a loved one when you hear something similar from the person you are listening to
- Picture the other's trauma happening in your environment

All of these types of visualization will increase the risky side of empathy for you.

While I would most highly suggest that you find ways not to visualize, short of that, the most helpful thing you can do is to make sure that any visualization is in the third person, that is, you are the observer and not the victim. It will also help to imagine an environment that means nothing at all personal to you. In general, make the visualization as far from anything that could personally impact you as possible.

An additional way to decrease the impact of visualization is by playing with the characteristics of the visualization: size, color, distance, and so on. In neurolinguistic programming (as discussed in Chapter 8) they call these submodalities (Bandler, 1985). Imagine your images on a screen and then manipulate the size of the screen and its distance from you. You can also change the picture from color to black and white or sepia and white, and so on. Do the same thing with sounds: play them forward, backward, louder, softer, slower, faster, and so on. By manipulating the submodalities, you learn that it is you who controls the images. Such mastery is integral to decreasing empathy's sting.

References

American Psychiatric Association. (1980). Diagnostic and statistical manual of mental disorders (3rd ed.). Washington, DC: Author.

American Psychiatric Association. (2000). Diagnostic and statistical manual of mental disorders (4th ed., text rev.). Washington, DC: Author.

Andrews, G., Slade, T., & Peters, L. (1999). Classification in psychiatry: ICD-10 versus DSM-IV. British Journal of Psychiatry, 174, 3–5.

Bandler, R. (1985). Using your brain—for a change. Moab, UT: Real People Press.

Bremner, J. D., Southwick, S., Brett, E., Fontana, A., Rosenheck, R., & Charney, D. S. (1992). Dissociation and posttraumatic stress disorder in Vietnam combat veterans. American Journal of Psychiatry, 149, 328–332.

Breslau, N. (2002). Gender differences in trauma and posttraumatic stress disorder. Journal of Gender Specific Medicine, 5(1), 34–40.

Breslau, N., Davis, G. C., Andreski, P., & Peterson, E. (1991). Traumatic events and posttraumatic stress disorder in an urban population of young adults. Archives of General Psychiatry, 48(3), 216–222.

Briere, J., Scott, C., & Weathers, F. (2005). Peritraumatic and persistent dissociation in the presumed etiology of PTSD. American Journal of Psychiatry, 162, 2295–2301.

Brunet, A., Orr, S. P., Tremblay, J., Robertson, K., Nader, K., & Pitman, R. K. (2008). Effect of post-retrieval propranolol on psychophysiologic responding during subsequent script-driven traumatic imagery in post-traumatic stress. Journal of Psychiatric Research, 42, 503–506.

Classen, C., Koopman, C., & Spiegel, D. (1993). Trauma and dissociation. Bulletin of the Menninger Clinic, 57, 178–194.

Damasio, A. R. (1994). Descartes' error. New York: Putnam.

Devilly, G. J. (2003). Psychological debriefing and the workplace: defining a concept, controversies, and guidelines for intervention. Australian Psychologist, 38(2), 144–150.

Diamond, R. J. (2009). Instant pharmacology (3rd ed.). New York: Norton.

Elliott, D. M. (1997). Traumatic events: Prevalence and delayed recall in the general population. Journal of Consulting and Clinical Psychology, 65, 811–820.

Emerson, D., Sharma, R., Chaudhry, S., & Turner, J. (2009). Trauma-sensitive yoga: Principles, practice, and research. International Journal of Yoga Therapy, 19, 123–128.

Famularo, R., Kinscherff, R., & Fenton, T. (1988). Propranolol Treatment for childhood posttraumatic stress disorder, acute type. American Journal of Diseases of Children, 142, 1244–1247.

Figley, C. R. (1995). Compassion fatigue: Coping with secondary traumatic stress disorder in those who treat the traumatized. New York: Brunner/Mazel.

Foa, E. B. (1993). Treating the trauma of rape: cognitive-behavioral therapy for PTSD. New York: Guilford.

Foa, E. B., & Kozak, J. J. (1986). Emotional processing of fear: Exposure to corrective information. Psychological Bulletin, 99, 20–35.

Frans, O., Rimmo, P. A., Aberg, L., & Fredrikson, M. (2005). Trauma exposure and post-traumatic stress disorder in the general population. Acta Psychiatrica Scandinavica, 111, 291–299.

Freudenberger, H. J. (1974). Staff burnout. Journal of Social Issues, 30, 159–165.

Gallese, V., Fadiga, L., Fogassi, L., & Rizzolatti, G. (1996). Action recognition in the premotor cortex. Brain, 119, 593–609.

Gunderson, J. G., Sabo, A. N. (1993). The phenomenological and conceptual interface between borderline personality disorder and PTSD. American Journal of Psychiatry, 150, 19–27.

Herman, J. L., & van der Kolk, B. A. (1987). Traumatic antecedents of BPD. In van der Kolk, B. A. (Ed.), Psychological Trauma (pp. 111–126). Washington, DC: American Psychiatric Press.

Holbrook, T. L., Galarneau, M. R., Dye, J. L., Quinn, K., & Dougherty, A. L. (2010). Morphine use after combat injury in Iraq and post-traumatic stress disorder. New England Journal of Medicine, 362, 110–117.

Huff, D. (1954). How to lie with statistics. New York: Norton.

Janet, P. (1898). Le traitement psychologique de l'hysterie. In A. Robin (Ed.), Traite de therapeutique appliquee. Paris: Rueff.

Janet, P. (1919). Les medications psychologiques (Vol. 3). Paris: Felix Alcan. (Reprint: New York: Arno Press, 1976)

Kabat-Zinn, J. (1990). Full catastrophe living. New York: Delta.

Kubetin, S. K. (2003). 20% dropout rate hinders prolonged therapy. Clinical Psychiatry News, 31(1), 54.

Kulka, R. A., Schlenger, W. E., Fairbank, J. A., Hough, R. L., Jordan, B. K., Marmar, C. R., et al., (1990). Trauma and the Vietnam war generation: Report of findings from the National Vietnam Veterans Readjustment Study. New York: Brunner/Mazel.

Lambert, M. J, & Barley, D. E. (2001). Research summary on the therapeutic relationship and psychotherapy outcome. Psychotherapy: Theory, Research, Practice, Training, 38, 357–361.

LeDoux, J. E. (1996). The emotional brain. New York: Touchstone.

Marshall, G. N., & Schell, T. L. (2002). Reappraising the link between peritraumatic dissociation and PTSD symptom severity: Evidence from a longitudinal study of community violence survivors. Journal of Abnormal Psychology, 111, 626–636.

Maslow, A. (1954). Motivation and personality. New York: Harper & Row.

McCann, L., & Pearlman, L. A. (1990). Vicarious traumatization: A framework for understanding the psychological effects of working with victims. Journal of Traumatic Stress, 3, 131–149.

Miller, J. J., Fletcher, K., & Kabat-Zinn, J. (1995). Three-year follow-up and clinical implications of a mindfulness meditation-based stress reduction intervention in the treatment of anxiety disorders. General Hospital Psychiatry, 17, 192–200.

Mitchell, J. T. (1985). CISD: Critical incident stress debriefing: Techniques of debriefing a[videotape]. Naples, FL: American Safety Video Publishers.

Mitchell, J. T. (1986). Critical incident stress management. Response, September/October, 24–25.

Ozer, E. J., Best, S. R., Lipsey, T. L., & Weiss, D. S. (2003). Predictors of posttraumatic stress disorder and symptoms in adults: A meta-analysis. Psychological Bulletin, 129, 52–73.

Perry, B. D. (1996). The neurobiology of adaptation and use-dependent development of the brain: How states become traits. Infant Mental Health Journal, 259, 271–291.

Pitman, R. K., Sanders, K. M., Zusman, R. M., Healy, A. R., Cheema,

F., Lasko, N. B., et al. (2002). Pilot study of secondary prevention of posttraumatic stress disorder with propranolol. Biological Psychiatry, 51, 189–142.

Reich, W. (1942). The function of the orgasm. New York: Orgone Institute Press.

Robinson, R. (2008). Reflections on the debriefing debate. International Journal of Emergency Mental Health, 10(4), 253–259.

Rothschild, B. (2000). The body remembers: The psychophysiology of trauma and trauma treatment. New York: Norton.

Rothschild, B. (2003). The body remembers Casebook: Unifying methods and models in the treatment of trauma and PTSD. New York: Norton.

Rothschild, B., with Rand, M. (2006). Help for the helper. New York: Norton.

Rothschild, B. (2010a). 8 keys to safe trauma recovery: Take-charge strategies to empower your healing. New York: Norton.

Rothschild, B. (2010b). Pearls from the early days of PTSD studies. In M. Kerman (Ed.), Clinical pearls of wisdom: 21 leading therapists offer their key insights (pp. 57–66). New York: Norton.

Schore, A. (2002). Dysregulation of the right brain: A Fundamental mechanism of traumatic attachment and the psychopathogenesis of posttraumatic stress disorder. Australian and New Zealand Journal of Psychiatry, 36, 9–30.

Schulte-Markwort, M., Marutt, K., & Riedesser, P. (Eds.). (2003). Cross-walks ICD-10/DSM-IV-TR: A synopsis of classifications of mental disorders. Cambridge, MA: Hogrefe Publishing.

Selye, H. (1984). The stress of life. New York: McGraw-Hill. (Original work published in 1956)

Siegel, D. (2007). The mindful brain. New York: Norton.

Siegel, D. (2010). The mindful therapist. New York: Norton.

Simon, G. E, Savarino, J., Operskalski, B., & Wang, P. S. (2006). Suicide risk during antidepressant treatment. American Journal of Psychiatry, 163, 41–47.

Tolin, F. D., & Foa, E. B (2002). Gender and PTSD: A cognitive model. In R. Kimerling, P. Ouimette, & J. Wolfe, (Eds.) Gender and PTSD (pp.76–97). New York: Guilford.

Watters, E. (2010). Crazy like us: The globalization of the American psyche. New York: Free Press.

Wolpe, J. (1969). The practice of behavior therapy. New York: Pergamon.

World Health Organization. (2007). ICD-10 online. http://apps.who. int/classifications/apps/icd/icd10online/.

Yehuda, R., & Golier, J. (2009). Is there a rationale for cortisol-based treatments for PTSD? Expert Review of Neurotherapeutics, 9, 1113–1115.

Yehuda, R., Kahana, B., Binder-Brynes, K., Southwick, S., Zemelman, S., Mason, J. W., et al. (1995). Low urinary cortisol excretion in Holocaust survivors with posttraumatic stress disorder. American Journal of Psychiatry, 152, 982–986.

Yehuda, R., Southwick, S. M., Nussbaum, G., Wahby, V., Giller, E. L. Jr., & Mason, J. W. (1990). Low urinary cortisol excretion in patients with posttraumatic stress disorder. Journal of Nervous and Mental Disease, 178, 366–369.

Yehuda, R., Teicher, M. H., Levengood, R., Trestman, R., & Siever, L. J. (1996). Cortisol regulation in posttraumatic stress disorder and major depression: A chronobiological analysis. Biological Psychiatry, 40, 79–88.

Index

A

abuse, substance. see substance abuse
accident(s), traumatic, 19
acute stress disorder (ASD), 23
  described, 25
  vs. other diagnoses in DSM, 25–26
adrenaline, 33–34, 33n
Ahsen, A., 76
Alcoholics Anonymous, 30
Alexander technique, 101
alpha-blockers, for PTSD, 87
American Journal of Psychiatry, 66
American Psychological Association (APA), 9, 23
amygdala, in information processing, 36–37
anticipation, in PTSD prevention, 120–21
antidepressants, for PTSD, 86
anxiety, levels of, 108
anxiety disorders, PTSD and, 27–28
APA. see American Psychological Association (APA)
arousal, contact and support lower, 129
ASD. see acute stress disorder (ASD)
attachment, PTSD and, 51–52
attachment disorder, PTSD and, 29
avoidance, in trauma therapy, 72

B

BA. see bodynamic analysis (BA)
Beck, A., 74
benzodiazepines, for PTSD, 86
beta-blockers, for PTSD, 86, 87
body therapies, nonpsychological, 81–82
bodynamic analysis (BA), 77
Bodynamic running technique (BRT), 77
borderline personality disorder (BPD), PTSD and, 28
BPD. see borderline personality disorder (BPD)
brain, psychological trauma effects on, 33–37
Brett, case study, 17–19, 26, 30–31, 44–45, 55, 82–83, 98, 103, 110–111, 118–119, 130
BRT. see Bodynamic running technique (BRT)
burnout, defined, 133
busipirone, for PTSD, 87

C

CBT. see cognitive-behavioral therapy (CBT)
central nervous system (CNS), psychological trauma effects on, 37–39

CISD. see controversial debriefing (CISD)
client(s)
    individual differences of, 15–16
    resources of, 14
    safety of, 13
client/therapist relationship, in trauma therapy, 13–14
CNS. see central nervous system (CNS)
cognitive therapies, 74
cognitive-behavioral therapy (CBT), 74–75
compassion fatigue, 133
control, in PTSD, 112–13
controversial debriefing (CISD), 130
cortex, psychological trauma effects on, 33–34
cortisol
    psychological trauma and, 39–40
    for PTSD, 85
Couric, K., 114
craniosacral technique, 101
Crazy Like Us: The Globalization of the American Psyche, 53
culture
    integration with, 60–61
    PTSD and, 53–54
curling parent, 51

D
Damasio, A., 10, 77
DBT. see dialectical behavior therapy (DBT)
debriefing, controversial, 130
defense(s), as resources, 14
Descartes' Error, 10
Diagnostic and Statistical Manual of Mental Disorders (DSM-III), 9
    on PTSD, 19
Diagnostic and Statistical Manual of Mental Disorders (DSM-IV-TR), on PTSD, 19
Diagnostic and Statistical Manual

of Mental Disorders (DSM), on PTSD, 23–24
Diagnostic and Statistical Manual of Mental Disorders (DSM-IV-TR), on trauma, 46
dialectical behavior therapy (DBT), 75
Diamond, R.J., 85
dissociation, peritraumatic, 47–48
dissociative disorder, PTSD and, 28
Dissociative Experiences Scale, 63
dual awareness, 38, 125
dual diagnosis, 29, 30

E
earthquakes, in Haiti (2010), 46–47, 51, 126
8 Keys to Safe Trauma Recovery, 114
EMDR. see eye movement desensitization and reprocessing (EMDR)
emotional freedom technique, 79
emotional support
    CISD, 130
    contact and support lower arousal, 129
    essential, 127–28
    out of isolation, 129
empathy, 135–38
    benefits of, 136
    decreasing sting of, 137–38
    described, 135
    neuroscience of, 135–36
    risks of, 136–37
energy therapies, 79
equine-assisted psychotherapy, 81
European and International Societies for Traumatic Stress Studies, 9
evidence-based treatment, for PTSD, 64–66
explicit memory, 43–44
exposure, prolonged, 75
expressive therapies, 81

eye movement desensitization and reprocessing (EMDR), 78–79, 115

F
false memory risk, 115–17
False Memory Syndrome Foundation, 116
family, integration with, 60–61
fatigue, compassion, 133
fear, friendly, 124–25
Feldenkrais technique, 101
fight response, to trauma, 20–21
Figley, C., 133
first aid, 126–31
   case examples, 130–31
   CISD, 130
   contact and support lower arousal, 129
   essential emotional support, 127–28
   invoking Maslow, 126–27
   out of isolation, 129
flight response, to trauma, 20
freeze response, to trauma, 21
Freud, S., 74
Full Catastrophe Living, 124

G
gender, as factor in PTSD, 52–53
Goodman, T., 97
group therapy, in PTSD therapy, 66–67
guilt, in PTSD, 114–15

H
Haiti, earthquakes in (2010), 46–47, 51, 126
hatha yoga, 99–100
helicopter parent, 51
Help for the Helper, 135
hippocampus, in information processing, 36–37
hovering parent, 51

How to Lie with Statistics, 69–70
Huff, D., 70
Hurricane Katrina, 126
hypnosis, 81

I
imagery, vulnerability and, 138–40
implicit memory, 42–43
Indian Ocean tsunami, of December 2004, 51, 126
information processing, pathways for, 36–37
Insight LA, 97
insurance, for PTSD therapy costs, 61–62
International Classification of Diseases, Classification of Mental and Behavioural Disorders, 23
isolation, out of, 129

J
Janet, P., 56–57
Jeffrey, case study, 10, 18–19, 26, 30, 31, 44, 55, 82–83, 98, 103, 110–111, 118–119, 130–131
Jung, C., 74

K
Kabat-Zinn, J., 124
Kurtz, R., 77

L
LeDoux, J., 36, 77
Levine, P., 76, 77
limbic system, psychological trauma effects on, 34–36

M
Marcher, L., 77
Maslow, A., 126–27
meditation, 94–98
   background of, 90
   calm vs. relaxed, 97
   case examples, 98

choosing focus in, 97
described, 94
eyes open or closed during, 96
mindfulness and, 90–91
physical position in classification
    of, 95
types of, 94–95
where to sit during, 96
memory(ies)
    explicit, 43–44
    implicit, 42–43
    normal, 41–44
    traumatic, 41–45. see also
        posttraumatic stress disorder
        (PTSD); traumatic memory
mindfulness, 90–94
    applying, 92–94
    background of, 90
    case examples, 92–94, 98
    described, 91–92
    means to developing, 91–92
    meditation and, 90–91
    trauma therapist and, 97–98
    for traumatized persons, 96
Mindfulness Based Stress Reduction,
    124
mirror neurons, 135–36
mirtazapine, for PTSD, 86
Mitchell, J., 130, 131
morphine, for PTSD, 87–88
motor nervous system, psychological
    trauma effects on, 38–39

N
Narcotics Anonymous, 30
natural events, traumatic, 19
nervous system, healing process of,
    109–10
neurolinguistic programming, 78,
    83, 139
neurons, mirror, 135–36
nonpsychological body therapies,
    81–82
noradrenaline, 33–34, 33n

O
Ogden, P., 77
ongoing trauma, 117–18
out of isolation, 129

P
panic attacks, PTSD and, 27–28
peritraumatic dissociation, 47–48
Perry, B., 53
person-to-person events, traumatic,
    19
phased treatment, 56–61
    Phase I, 57
    Phase II, 58
    Phase III, 60
physical therapy, 101
pilates, 101
planning, in PTSD prevention,
    120–21
Porges, S., 77
posttraumatic stress disorder
    (PTSD), 22–26
    anxiety disorders and, 27–28
    attachment and, 51–52
    attachment disorder and, 29
    avoidance in, 72
    BPD and, 28
    case examples, 17–18, 22–23, 26,
        30, 46–47, 55, 118–19
    common issues inherent in,
        112–19
    conditions associated with, 27–30
    control in, 112–13
    culture and, 53–54
    defined, 24–25
    dissociative disorder and, 28
    DSM on, 23–24, 46
    examples of, 22–23
    false memory risk in, 115–17
    gender as factor in, 52–53
    guilt in, 114–15
    hallmark of, 41
    incidence of, 25
    memory distortion in, 41

panic attacks and, 27–28
peritraumatic dissociation, 47–48
predilection for, 46–55
prevention of, 120–25. see also
    posttraumatic stress disorder
    (PTSD) prevention
response to, 46–47
shame in, 114–15
stress as core of, 32–33
substance abuse and, 29
support in, 113–14
TBI and, 29–30
terminology related to, 23–24
trauma history and, 48–50
treatment of, 56–67. see also
    specific methods and post-
    traumatic stress disorder
    (PTSD) therapy
vs. other diagnoses in DSM, 25–26
vulnerability to, 55
posttraumatic stress disorder
    (PTSD) prevention
anticipation in, 120–21
friendly fear in, 124–25
planning in, 120–21
prebriefing in, 123
rehearsal in, 122–23
self-defense training in, 124
stress management in, 124
posttraumatic stress disorder
    (PTSD) therapy, 56–67.
    see also specific medications and
    trauma therapy
alpha-blockers, 87
antidepressants, 86
benzodiazepines, 86
beta-blockers, 86, 87
busipirone, 87
evaluating individual needs in,
    63–64
evidence-based treatment in,
    64–66
focus of, 71–73
group therapy in, 66–67

integration with family and
    culture in normal daily life in,
    60–61
interpreting research on, 69–71
mirtazapine, 86
models for, 68–83. see also specific
    types and trauma therapy
morphine, 87–88
phased treatment in, 56–61
psychopharmacology, 84–89. see
    also specific medications and
    psychopharmacology
remembering and processing
    trauma memories in, 58–60
safety in, 57–58
short- vs. long-term, 61–64
sleeping pills, 88–89
SNRIs, 86
SSRIs, 86
stabilization in, 57–58
success of, 71
therapeutic relationship in, 64
who pays for it, 61–62
prebriefing, in PTSD prevention, 123
prevention, PTSD, 120–25. see also
    posttraumatic stress disorder
    (PTSD) prevention
professional(s), self-care for, 134–35
programming, neurolinguistic, 78
prolonged exposure, 75
psychoanalysis, 80
psychodynamic psychotherapy,
    80–82
psychological trauma, 17–21. see also
    specific types, e.g. posttraumatic
    stress disorder (PTSD)
body effects of, 37–39
brain effects of, 33–37
case examples, 33
categories of, 19
CNS effects of, 37–39
cortex effects of, 33–34
cortisol and, 39–40
impact of, 18

limbic system effects of, 34–36
motor nervous system effects of, 38–39
sensory nervous system effects of, 37–38
stress and, 18–20
psychopharmacology
  alpha-blockers, 87
  antidepressants, 86
  benzodiazepines, 86
  beta-blockers, 86, 87
  busipirone, 87
  cortisol, 85
  mirtazapine, 86
  morphine, 87–88
  for PTSD, 84–89
  sleeping pills, 88–89
  SNRIs, 86
  SSRIs, 86
psychotherapy(ies)
  equine-assisted, 81
  psychodynamic, 80–82
  somatic, 76
  traditional methods of, 79–80
PTSD. see posttraumatic stress disorder (PTSD)

R
Red Cross, 126
Red Cross lifeguard course, 134
rehearsal, in PTSD prevention, 122–23
Reich, W., 76
relaxation training, 101
research, on trauma therapy, 69–71
research bias, in PTSD therapy, 70–71
research subjects, in PTSD therapy, 71
resource(s)
  of clients, 14
  for taking trauma history, 50
Rolf, I., 76
rolfing, 101

S
safety
  in PTSD therapy, 57–58
  in trauma therapy, 13
Schore, A., 53
selective serotonin reuptake inhibitors (SSRIs), for PTSD, 86
self-care
  for professionals, 134–35
  vulnerability and, 132–40
self-defense training, in PTSD prevention, 124
Selye, H., 19, 32
sensory motor processing, 77
sensory nervous system, psychological trauma effects on, 37–38
September 11, 2001, World Trade Center attacks of, 51, 88, 109, 126
serotonin norepinephrine reuptake inhibitors (SNRIs), for PTSD, 86
shame, in PTSD, 114–15
Shapiro, F., 78
Siegel, D., 77, 90
60 Minutes, 114
sleeping pills, for PTSD, 88–89
SNRIs. see serotonin norepinephrine reuptake inhibitors (SNRIs)
somatic experiencing, 76–77
somatic psychotherapies, 76
somatic trauma therapy (STT), 77–78
somatic treatment adjuncts, 99–103
  Alexander technique, 101
  case examples, 103
  craniosacral technique, 101
  Feldenkrais technique, 101
  physical therapy, 101
  pilates, 101
  relaxation training, 101
  rolfing, 101
  strength training, 102–3
  yoga, 99–100
SSRIs. see selective serotonin reuptake inhibitors (SSRIs)

stabilization, in PTSD therapy, 57–58
strength training, 102–3
stress
    as core of PTSD, 32–33
    defined, 18–19
    examples of, 19
    traumatic, 18–20
stress inoculation, 51
stress management, in PTSD
    prevention, 124
STT. see somatic trauma therapy
    (STT)
Subjective Anxiety Scale, 108
subjective unit of disturbance (SUD),
    108
submodalities, 139–40
substance abuse, PTSD and, 29
SUD (subjective unit of disturbance),
    108
SUD scale (SUDS), 108
SUDS. see SUD scale (SUDS)
Sullenberger, C. "Sully," 114, 122
support, in PTSD, 113–14

T
TBI. see traumatic brain injury (TBI)
The Body Remembers, 13, 77
The Body Remembers Casebook, 13
The Miracle on the Hudson, 122
The Stress of Life, 19
theory, knowledge of, 15
therapeutic relationship, in PTSD
    therapy, 64
therapist(s)
    mindfulness and, 97–98
    preparation of, 16
    self-care for, 134–35
therapist/client relationship, in
    trauma therapy, 13–14
thought field therapy, 79
transactional analysis, 80–81
trauma
    defined, 46
    DSM-IV-TR on, 46

group therapy for, 66–67
history taking following, 48–50
normal response to, 20–21
ongoing, 117–18
psychological, 17–21. see also
    psychological trauma
triggers for, 107–8
trauma history, 48–50
    resources for, 50
trauma memory. see traumatic
    memory(ies)
trauma system, as pressure cooker,
    15
trauma therapy. see also
    posttraumatic stress disorder
    (PTSD) therapy
avoidance in, 72
BA, 77
BRT, 77
case examples, 82–83, 110–11
CBT, 74–75
client's individual differences in,
    15–16
client's internal and external
    resources, 14
client's view of, 105–6
cognitive therapies, 74
current methods of, 68–83
DBT, 75
defenses as resources in, 14
EMDR, 78–79
emotional freedom technique, 79
energy therapies, 79
equine-assisted psychotherapy, 81
expressive therapies, 81
focus of, 71–73
foundations for, 13–16
goal of, 104–5
goals of, 9–10
hypnosis, 81
interpreting research on, 69–71
knowledge of theory in, 15
nervous system healing process,
    109–10

neurolinguistic programming, 78
nonpsychological body therapies,
  81–82
objective evaluation criteria in,
  108–9
as pressure cooker, 15
prolonged exposure, 75
psychoanalysis, 80
psychodynamic psychotherapy,
  80–82
safety in, 13
sensory motor processing, 77
somatic, 77–78
somatic experiencing, 76–77
somatic psychotherapies, 76
specialized, 78
subjective evaluation criteria, 109
success criteria, 71, 104–11
symptom profile at outset of, 106–7
therapist/client relationship in,
  13–14
therapist's preparation in, 16
thought field therapy, 79
traditional methods of
  psychotherapy, 79–80
transactional analysis, 80–81
traumatic incident reduction, 79
trauma triggers, 107–8
traumatic brain injury (TBI), PTSD
  and, 29–30
traumatic events, 18
  categories of, 19

traumatic incident reduction, 79
traumatic memory(ies)
  case examples, 44–45
  described, 41–45
  remembering and processing,
    58–60
traumatic stress, vs. other forms of
  stress, 18–20
traumatized persons, mindfulness
  for, 96
trigger(s), trauma-related, 107–8
tsunami, Indian Ocean, 51, 126

V
van der Kolk, B., 77
vulnerability, 132–40
  described, 133–34
  empathy and, 135–38
  imagery and, 138–40
  self-care and, 132–40

W
Watters, E., 53
Wolpe, J., 74, 108
World Health Organization, 23
World Trade Center attacks, of
  September 11, 2001, 51, 88, 109,
  126

Y
Yehuda, R., 39, 85
yoga, 99–100